REFLEC

Images of Britis
their own w

REFLECTIONS

Images of British women in their own words

Mary Gifford Brown

Hutchinson

London · Melbourne · Sydney · Auckland · Johannesburg

Hutchinson Education
An imprint of Century Hutchinson Ltd
62–65 Chandos Place, London WC2N 4NW

Century Hutchinson Australia Pty Ltd
PO Box 496, 16–22 Church Street, Hawthorn,
Victoria 3122, Australia

Century Hutchinson New Zealand Ltd
PO Box 40–086, Glenfield, Auckland 10,
New Zealand

Century Hutchinson South Africa (Pty) Ltd
PO Box 337, Berglvei 2012, South Africa

First published 1988

Set in Linotron 11/12 Sabon by
Input Typesetting Ltd, London SW19 8DR

Printed and bound in Great Britain by
Anchor Brendon Ltd, Tiptree, Essex

British Library Cataloguing in Publication Data

Images of British women.
1. English literature—Women authors
I. Brown, Mary Gifford
820.8'09287 PR1110.W6

ISBN 0 09 173185 2

Contents

Acknowledgements

I am very grateful to my husband Francis James Brown for all the interest he has given me in selecting the material for this book and to my daughter Suzanna for her helpful criticism; I owe my thanks to Barbara Halton, Francis Gosse and Stella Gordon in Athens for their secretarial skills; my special gratitude goes to my friend and legal adviser, the Right Honourable Lord Fletcher of Islington for all his valuable support and encouragement.

The author and publishers would like to thank the Copyright holders below for their kind permission to reproduce the following material:
Allen & Unwin for 'The year one' by Kathleen Raine from *Collected Poems of Kathleen Raine.*
Central Independent Television plc for two extracts from an interview given by the Prime Minister, Margaret Thatcher in June 1986.
Chatto & Windus for an extract from *A Life of One's Own* by Joanna Field.
Andre Deutsch for an extract from *Marie Stopes* by Ruth Hall.
Hamlyn for a poem entitled 'War Girls' by Jesse Pope, taken from the Anthology '*Scars Upon My Heart*', by Catherine Reilly.
Virago Press Ltd for an extract from *Novel on Yellow Paper* by Stevie Smith, copyright © James MacGibbon 1936, first published by Jonathan Cape Ltd 1936, reprinted with permission from Virago Press Ltd (1980), and for 'Meditation at Kew' and 'The Fired Pot' by Anna Wickham from *The Writings of Anna Wickham* edited by R D Smith, copyright © James and George Helpburn 1984, published by Virago Press Ltd 1980.

Acknowledgements

The Trustees of the British Museum for plates 1, 2, 3, 7 and 12; The Fine Art Society for plate 9; the Mistress and Fellows, Girton College, Cambridge for plate 11; The Imperial War Museum for plate 10; Sara and Ben John for plate 8; The Tate Gallery for plates 4, 5 and 14; and The Victoria and Albert Museum for plates 6 and 13.

Foreword

Though this is a book about women and by women, it is not a 'feminist tract.' Great women writers, like great men writers, are universal and entertain while they teach. Mary Gifford Brown has found an enormous variety of material – some from well known writers like Jane Austen, Edith Sitwell and Margaret Drabble, some from women whose positions in life set them apart – Queen Victoria, Elizabeth I, Elizabeth Fry. There are extracts from the writings of women who travelled and women who stayed at home. There is a particularly enchanting diary entry from an eight year old who lived at the beginning of the nineteenth century.

I think this is a book for enjoying. Extracts from books one has read remind one of the pleasure of the whole; extracts from those one has not read should send one scurrying to the nearest library, for it is obvious that women have been as busy with their pens as with their needles over the centuries. Most of these writers seem to me to be possessed of enormous sympathy and humour as well as great strength of character and acute powers of observation. Mary Gifford Brown has linked together these extracts succinctly and stylishly.

This is a most welcome book and will, I hope, introduce new readers to some marvellous writing, in addition to showing us ourselves as we see us.

Judi Dench

Introduction

During my frequent invitation tours in the United States and elsewhere I was often asked whether the material I was using was available in a collected, published form. I had to reply that it was not. I was giving dramatised readings from works of, or about, British women to university students and to mixed audiences at meetings organised by the English Speaking Union, The British Council, and institutions interested in Women's Studies. The material ranged across several centuries and was representative of women of all ages with varying backgrounds of education, experience and achievement. Each passage reflected an aspect of British women that had fascinated me and provided a rich source of material for the discussions and study that often followed my readings. Each item was designed, either through its authorship or subject matter, to contribute in some way to an understanding of the place of British women in the social history of Britain and in the evolution of our country's literary, intellectual, artistic and spiritual progress.

It is in response to these calls for a publication of my selected passages that I offer this volume in the form of an anthology. Any anthology requires a word of explanation. It is an entirely personal selection. It does not attempt an academic critique of British women's literary or other achievements. Nor does it attempt to portray any composite patterns or image of British womanhood. That would be an impossible task. All British women have their own unique characteristics and the individual reader must be left to form his or her own image of those who contribute to this anthology. There is more diversity than unity. But what I do offer, however, is a rich mosaic of experiences of British women taken from their letters, diaries, journals and autobiographies, or from their novels, biographies, poetry and plays. There are glimpses of woman responding to her circumstances in youth; in love, marriage and motherhood; in her search for self-fulfilment; and in her old age.

I have limited my selection to British women because, being British myself, I feel a certain bond in our shared heritage. As this anthology is often used in dramatised readings all over the world, my own very British accent gives extra colour and authenticity to the chosen extracts. They do not follow each other in chronological order; rather the excerpts are arranged in what I hope is a logical sequence according to their content. It struck me when gathering the material for this anthology that the similarities, dissimilarities and links between the passages had little or nothing to do with their sequence in time.

I know that many of the quotations will strike a familiar and sympathetic chord with the reader, as they have with me. To other readers they will offer a new perspective, a new line of thought that will, I hope, lead to a stimulating dialogue as was the case with the students who came to my readings. I have endeavoured to encourage this by including in some of the introductory paragraphs my own observations and reflections in the quoted passages as a foil for the attention of the reader.

I assembled the first pieces of this book – classic passages from Jane Austen – many years ago, to introduce young and adult audiences in Nigeria to the best of British literature. I spent five years there, bringing up my own young family and teaching for two and a half years at Adeyemi College of Education, Ondo. During that time I combed every library shelf, as well as all my friends' bookshelves, for material which would give my students at least an awareness of the tremendous scope and richness of our islands' literary heritage – and the contribution which women had made to this. When I was asked to tour the United States, I found there an avid interest in the achievements of British women, an interest beyond literature. This caused my collection to grow in size and variety to include the experiences of British women in the wider social, political and artistic arenas.

It is a tribute to their achievements that I have found this scale of interest everywhere I have been invited to give my readings, most recently in Greece where my husband and I have our home. It is there that this book has taken shape; there that I have reviewed the material from which these quotations are selected, enjoying again their impact and regretting only that so many others have had to be omitted! My hope is that those I have chosen will provide some new experiences of the lives and works of British women.

Plate 1 From an original drawing by the Princess Victoria given by Her Royal Highness to the Duchess of Kent on 17th August, 1831

1

In youth

Among the images I have chosen in this first section, I have found a unity of experience spanning centuries. These early years of girlhood have always presented us with charm and beauty. It is the time for fresh curiosity, spirited hope, uncompromising standards, aspirations and dreams, fears and disappointments too. However far we have come, so much, good and bad, remains the same.

Each generation seems to set ideals and standards for its successors, and bequeaths to its youth the task of building the future: certainly as a young adolescent at the end of the Second World War I felt, along with my contemporaries, the weight of expectation, of responsibility put on us to reshape a shattered world. Now, a generation later, I cannot help wondering how the youth of today can overcome the huge threat of destruction and universal termination which has overshadowed their childhood. How can they, in this shadow, pursue their personal and natural aspirations to create, to preserve, and to go forward? If it is anywhere, the inspiration for their task is in the natural hope and optimism of childhood, in its irresistible strength and resilience.

Mary Russell Mitford, writing in the 1820s, gives us a beautiful exposition of these qualities in a portrait of a child in her book Our Village:

Next door lives a carpenter, with his excellent wife, and their little daughter Lizzy, the plaything and queen of the village . . . She manages everybody in the place, her schoolmistress included . . . Seduces cakes and lollypops from the very shop window; makes the lazy carry her, the silent talk to her, the grave romp with her; does anything she pleases; is absolutely irresistible. Her chief attraction lies in her exceeding power of loving, and firm reliance on the love and indulgence of others . . . She has imperial attitudes too and loves to stand with her hands behind her or folded over her bosom; and sometimes, when she has a little touch of shyness, she clasps them together on the top of her head pressing down her shining curls, and looking so exquisitely pretty. Yes Lizzy is the queen of the village.

Mary Mitford needed much strength and resilience during her own childhood. She was the daughter of a country doctor whose extravagance wasted the family fortunes, forcing them to leave their beautiful country home to live in poor circumstances in a dingy house in London. Mary Mitford recalls all this in her Recollections of a Literary Life.

One remarkable incident from that childhood, on her tenth birthday, reads like a fairy tale: her father, Dr Mitford, liked to walk about London on his professional business with little Mary holding his hand. Sometimes they found their way to a lottery office. On that particular day Mary was determined she would have no other ticket than the number 2,224. It was bought for her, with some difficulty, and turned up the prize of £20,000! 'Ah me' reflects Miss Mitford, 'in less than twenty years, what was left of the produce of the ticket so strangely chosen? What, except a Wedgewood dinner service that my father had ordered to commemorate the event, with the Irish harp within the border on one side, and his family crest on the other? That fragile and perishable ware long outlasted the more perishable money. Then came long years of toil and struggle and anxiety, and jolting over the rough ways of the world, and although want often came very close to our door, it never actually entered.'

The Mitford family retired to a small cottage at Three Mile Cross near Reading in Berkshire and Mary lived there for thirty years. It was her need to earn a living as a writer that gave us, among other works, the world-famous collection of sketches and stories which is Our Village.

From the seventeenth century we have this description of another little girl, Lady Mary Montague, eldest daughter of the

Fifth Earl of Kingston and Lady Fielding, sister of the novelist Henry Fielding. This account was given by a contemporary eye-witness at the then fashionable Kit-Cat Club in London. The Kit-Cat Club was founded in 1700 and was composed of thirty-nine noblemen and gentlemen whose prime function as members was to toast the beauties of the day.

She went from the lap of one poet, or patriot, or statesman, to the arm of another. Was feasted with sweetmeats, overwhelmed with caresses, and what probably pleased her better than either, heard her wit and beauty loudly extolled on every side. 'Pleasure,' she said, 'was too poor a word to express her sensations, they amounted to ecstasy.' Never again throughout her whole future life did she pass so happy a day.

Lady Mary Montague was then eleven years old, displaying all the childhood powers of attraction and manipulation that we saw in Mary Mitford's Lizzy, but this time with the extra dimension of awareness of her own charms. Lady Mary grew up to be an adventuress and intrepid traveller, recording her exploits in a series of brilliant letters published in 1763.

The pure, evocative qualities of childhood are to be found everywhere in British literature, and have been used to great effect. Mary Braddon was credited by novelist Mrs Oliphant as being 'the inventor of the fair-haired demon of modern fiction'. Lucy Graham, this fragile blonde angel, becomes the would-be murderess in Mary Braddon's brilliant novel Lady Audley's Secret, *published in 1862:*

Wherever she went she seemed to take joy and brightness with her. In the cottages of the poor her fair face shone like a sunbeam. For you see Miss Lucy Graham was blessed with that magic power of fascination by which a woman can charm with a word or intoxicate with a smile. Everyone loved, admired and praised her. The boy who opened the five-barred gate that stood in her pathway ran home to tell his mother of her pretty looks, and the sweet voice in which she thanked him of the little service. The verger at the church who ushered her into the servant's pew; the vicar who saw the soft blue eyes uplifted to his face as he preached his simple sermons; the porter from the railway station who brought her sometimes a letter or a parcel and who never looked for a reward from her, her employers, his visitors, her pupils, their servants, everybody high and low, united in declaring that Lucy Graham was the sweetest girl that ever lived.

Some of the most vivid images we have of woman in childhood come from reminiscence: the pictures formed in adult minds from long-stored memories. One such picture, of Canfield Place, is given to us by Beatrix Potter in her journal, written between 1881 and 1897:

The pleasantest association of that pleasant room for me is of our teas there in the twilight. I hope I am not by nature greedy, but there was something rapturous to us London children in the unlimited supply of new milk. It came up warm in a great snuff-coloured jug which seemed to have no bottom and made the milk look blue. I seem to hear the chink of the crockery as the nurse girl brought it out of the closet in the wall and laid the coarse clean cloth. Then we had eggs, so new that the most perverse kitchen maid could not hard-boil them. There was not much furniture in that room. Some dwarf elbow chairs and a stumpy low table on which we made sand pies and sailed therein as a boat when wrong side up. When I was a child I once slipped on the sloping boards and sprained my wrists badly. But I bear no grudge for that, for it proved an excuse for breaking off piano lessons. The green curtains slid on a long brass pole. I know it was hollow for once we took it down to extract a tame field mouse.

From such rich observation came Peter Rabbit, The Tailor of Gloucester *and the other inimitable stories for children which Beatrix Potter began to write and illustrate as a young woman of twenty-seven, when she was writing a series of illustrated letters to a sick child. At the age of forty-seven she married William Heelis, a solicitor from Ambleside in Cumbria, and spent the last thirty years of her life sheep-farming in the Lake District.*

Another account of childhood is given in the memoirs of Lady Ann Fanshawe, written in the seventeenth century. She wrote these for her infant son to give him the story of her early life and happy marriage. In so doing, she has given us the most charming image of herself as a 'hoyting' girl, ('hoyting' or 'hoiting' describes a frolicsome, romping or flighty person), with the mixture of diligence and fun that is definitive of a child in any era.

I was educated with all the advantage that time afforded both for working all sorts of fine works with my needle, and learning French, singing, playing the lute and virginals, and dancing; and not withstanding I learned as well as most did, yet was I wild to that degree, that the hours of my beloved recreation took up too much of my time, for I loved horse-back riding in the first place, and running and all other active pastimes; and in fine I was that which we graver people call a hoyting girl. But to be just to myself, I never did mischief to myself or other people, nor one immodest action or word in my life; but skipping and activity was my delight.

Rather less definitive are the schooldays remembered by Jessica Mitford in the 1920s. She was one of the six famous, or rather infamous, children of that splendidly eccentric English couple, Lord and Lady Redesdale. In Daughters and Rebels *she recalls:*

I graduated to the schoolroom when I was nine. . . Miss Whitey taught us to repeat 'A-squared-minus-B-squared-equals-A-squared-minus-2-AB-plus-B-squared,' but she did not stay long enough to explain why that should be. Baud found out that she had a deadly fear of snakes, and left Enid, her pet grass snake, neatly wrapped around the W.C. chain one morning. We breathlessly awaited the result, which was not long in coming. Miss Whitey locked herself in, there was shortly an earsplitting shriek followed by a thud. The unconscious woman was ultimately released with the aid of crowbars, and Baud was duly scolded and told to keep Enid in her box thereafter. Miss Whitey was succeeded by Miss Broadmoor, who taught us to say *mensa, mensa, mensam* all the way through. Nancy, even in these early days, preoccupied with U and non-U usage, made up a poem illustrative of the main 'refainments' of Miss Broadmoor's speech: 'Ay huff a loft, and oft, as ay lay on may ayderdown so soft (tossing from sade to sade with may nasty coff) ay ayther think of the loft, or of the w-h-h-h-h-eat in the troff of the loft.' We couldn't resist reciting it each morning as lesson time drew near. Latin lessons came to an end after Miss

Broadmoor left. Miss McMurray grew beans on bits of wet flannel and taught the names of different parts of these growing beans – plumule, radical, embryo.

Jessica Mitford eloped with Sir Winston Churchill's nephew and lived a life of adventure, much of which is recorded in Daughters and Rebels. *The schooldays, so graphically recalled, were shared with sisters Unity, nicknamed Baud and later disciple of Hitler; Diana, married to English Fascist Sir Oswald Mosley; Nancy, well-known novelist; and Deborah, who became Duchess of Devonshire.*

The Mitford girls might well have thoroughly enjoyed the seventeenth-century convent establishments where young women, known as the Galloping Nuns, spent five or ten years under solemn vows of chastity. When their time expired, they could renew their contract, or marry, or pursue another way of life. Aphra Behn, writing in the second half of the seventeenth century, describes these establishments when introducing her heroine, the fair Miranda, in The Fair Jilt, *or* The Amours of Prince Tarquin and Miranda*:*

These Orders are taken up by the best persons of the town, young maidens of fortune, who live together not inclosed, under a sort of Abbess, or Prioress, or rather a Governante.

But as these women are, as I said, of the best quality, and live with the reputation of being retired from the world a little more than ordinary, and because there is a sort of difficulty to approach them, they are the people the most courted, and liable to the greatest temptations, for as difficult as it seems to be, they receive visits from all the men of the best quality, especially strangers. All the men of wit and conversation meet at the apartments of these fair *filles devotees* where all manner of gallantries are performed while all the study of these maids is to accomplish themselves for these noble conversations. They receive presents, balls, serenades, and *billets*. All the news, wit, verses, songs, novels, music, gaming, and all fine diversion is in all their apartments, they themselves being of the best quality and fortune. So that to manage these gallantries, there is no sort of female arts they are not practised in, no intrigue they are ignorant of, and no management of which they are not capable.

Edith Matilda, born in 1080 and later 'Good Queen Maud', was brought up at quite a different nunnery, the nunnery of Wilton, 'the most famous refuge of English noblewomen after the Conquest'. It was there, from 1086 until she was thirteen years of age, that her aunt Christina directed and disciplined her. Piety did not come easily, it seems, to the young girl:

I went in fear of the rod of my aunt Christina and she would often make me smart with a good slapping and the most horrible scolding, as well as treating me as being in disgrace.

Later she expressed her rage when aunt Christina insisted on her covering her head with a veil. She wrote:

I did indeed wear [it] in her presence but as soon as I was able to escape out of her sight I tore it off and threw it on the ground and trampled on it and in that way I used to vent my rage and hatred of it which boiled up in me.

Little girls today rebel just as much against authority as they did nine centuries ago. We find many of the experiences of growing up common to us all in every century.

Stevie Smith's recollections of Miss Hogmanimy, published in 1936 in her autobiographical Novel on Yellow Paper, *are within the experience of many:*

There was once a woman called Miss Hogmanimy . . . a queer name. That was a name you would certainly want to get married out of. But this woman was very queer and wrought up over babies and the way babies are born, and she gave up her whole life going round giving free lectures to young girls of school age or school-leaving age. And all the time it was mixed up with not drinking alcohol, but just carrying on on ginger beer and Kola and pop. And so, well, this Miss Hogmanimy she got up in our school, now I think it was our school chapel, giving a lecture with illustrating slides to young girls on how babies are born . . . But to listen to Miss Hogmanimy you'd think just knowing straight out how babies was born was to solve all the problems of adolescence right off. You'd come out straight and simple and full of hearty fellowship and right thinking if you just got it clear once and for all how babies are born. There'd be no more coming out in spots and getting self-conscious about the senior prefect, nor getting a crush on the English mistress, nor feeling proud and miserable like you do at that time before you get grown up. There'd be none of this at all if you just knew how babies are born. So there she was . . . And what did we get? First of all Miss Hogmanimy got a special way of speaking like losing her puff a bit in an uphill climb, it was very like this, a sort of breathless whisper that could yet be heard, I'll say this for her, she could be heard. But oh what nonsense she had to say, and how foiled we felt, my friend and I, because all she said was always Oh how beautiful it all is, and how it is the holiest thing on earth, and she would pray a prayer first of all, and we waited and waited, and hoped some time we would get the facts, but no it was all this funny breathless whisper . . . Well, the upshot of it all was she wanted us to sign a paper saying we would never drink anything but ginger beer and allied liquids. And she had a smile that was very cunning and deliberate. It came out like it was spontaneous, but somehow you knew it wasn't so-o-o spontaneous, but cleverly timed. And she said 'Now girls if you are at dinner and they offer you wine, don't make a fuss, we needn't make a fuss, but just say I don't take that, thank you.' And then she would enlarge upon how alcohol leads to irregularity in sexual behaviour. Oh, what a lovely phrase that is, and how it does not describe the way you feel at parties sometimes, if you have your right friends there, and that lovely feeling, oh how I enjoy it. But of course about this I did not learn until long after the day of Miss Hogmanimy.

I'm sure right up to the 1940s and beyond there were talcumed, delicate Miss Hogmanimys visiting the education establishments for young ladies in order to impart the facts of life – as they saw them. How well I remember the smell of nervous perspiration as I sat with my classmates, after hymns and prayers, listening to one such lady warning us – obliquely, of course – of the consequences of arousing the boys' 'baser passions'. It made me feel the boys must be protected. A far cry from the sex education lessons of today.

Apart from these very singular glimpses of the education of certain young women, there is a wealth of material on the wider subject. Some is aimed at presenting the 'ideal' young woman, setting standards and patterns by which she should behave and be measured.

Maria Edgeworth belonged to a group of women who were keen to do away with the vast inequalities of their sex and to lay down definite standards by which women should live. In her book Practical Education, *published in 1798, she writes:*

In the education of girls we must teach them more caution than is necessary to boys . . . they must trust to the experience of others, they cannot always have recourse to what ought to be, they must adapt themselves to what is.

We cannot help thinking that their happiness is of more consequence than their speculative rights, and we wish to educate women so that they may be happy in the situation in which they are most likely to be placed.

Girls must very soon perceive the impossibility of their rambling about the world in quest of adventures.

A just idea of the nature of dignity, opposed to what is commonly called spirit, should be given early to our female pupils.

So much depends upon the temper of women, that it ought to be most carefully cultivated in early life; girls should be more inured to restraint than boys, because they are more likely to meet with restraint in society.

To twentieth-century women, Maria Edgeworth is urging woman to put up with her lot rather than to fight for her equality, but her recognition of the need to develop girls' talents and capacities laid the foundation for later campaigns for equal education to be launched and won. Maria Edgeworth had much experience of adapting herself to her circumstances. From the age of fifteen she taught her eighteen brothers and sisters, and helped her landowner father run the family estate in Ireland. Throughout her life she wrote articles and books on education, and several novels which earned her considerable sums. Even at the age of eighty she was organising relief work during the Irish famine of 1846.

Writing at the same time, Mary Wollstonecraft, gifted educationalist, writer and feminist thinker, published in 1792 A

Vindication for the Rights of Women *which includes these excerpts on girls' upbringing. Her book was an attack on contemporary society and drew on her educational experiences and revolutionary ideas.*

In order to preserve health and beauty I should earnestly recommend frequent ablutions . . . girls ought to be taught to wash and dress alone, and if some of them should require a little assistance let it not be till that part of the business is over which ought never to be done before a fellow creature.

I object to many females being shut up together in nurseries, convents or boarding schools. I fear that here girls are first spoiled, particularly in the latter. I cannot recollect without indignation the jokes which knots of young women indulge themselves in. A number of girls sleep in the same room and wash together. And though I should be sorry to instill false delicacy I should be very anxious to prevent their acquiring nasty or immodest habits.

To say the truth women are in general too familiar with each other and that gross familiarity frequently renders the marriage state unhappy.

When friends meet in the morning I have been pleased after breathing the sweet bracing morning air, to see the same kind of freshness in the countenances I particularly loved. I was glad to see them braced as it were, for the day and ready to run their course with the sun. Nay I have often felt hurt . . . disgusted when a friend has appeared with her clothes huddled on, because she chose to indulge herself in bed till the last moment.

As a sex, women are habitually indolent and everything tends to make them so. O! my sisters ye must acquire that soberness of mind which the exercise of duties and the pursuit of knowledge alone inspire, or ye will be still remaining in a doubtful situation and only be loved whilst ye are fair.

Three-quarters of a century later Eliza Lynn Linton, novelist and journalist, waged a bitter campaign against 'modern phases of womanhood' which were antagonistic to her own ideas of feminine charm. An article in the Saturday Review *of 14 March 1868, entitled 'Girl of the Period', launched the campaign:*

A fair young English girl meant the ideal of womanhood to us, of home, birth and breeding. It meant a creature generous, capable, modest, something franker than a French woman, more to be trusted than an Italian, as brave as an American, but more refined, as domestic as a German and more graceful. It meant a girl that could be trusted alone if need be, because of the innate purity and dignity of her nature, but who was neither bold in nature nor masculine in mind.

The 'Girl of the Period' and the fair young English girl of the past have nothing in common save ancestry and their mother tongue. The 'Girl of the Period' is a creature who dyes her hair and paints her face – a creature whose sole idea of life is fun; whose sole aim is unbounded luxury and whose dress is the chief object of such thought and intellect as she possesses. The 'Girl of the Period' has done away with such moral muffishness as consideration for others or regard for counsel and rebuke. She lives to please herself and she does not care if she displeases everyone else.

These words might be thought apposite today by those who would castigate the habitués *of Chelsea's Kings Road!*

In Victorian times it can be said that girlhood was regarded as sacred. Much thought and many words were spent extolling maidens' virtues and recommending good practices. This anonymous verse is typical of the time:

> Be good sweet maid, and let who will be clever.
> Do noble things, not dream them all day long.
> And so make life, death and that vast forever
> One grand sweet song.

Queen Victoria was a pattern of decorum and dignity, as this excerpt from Fanny Kemble's Records of Later Life, Volume 1 *illustrates. She is recalling the first meeting between Queen Victoria and her Parliament when the Queen was just nineteen years old.*

The serene serious sweetness of her candid brow and clear soft eyes gave dignity to the girlish countenance, while the want of height only added to the effect of extreme youth of the round but slender person, and gracefully moulded hands and arms.

The Queen's voice was exquisite; nor have I ever heard any spoken words more musical in their gentle distinctness than the 'My Lords and Gentlemen' which broke the breathless silence of the illustrious assembly, whose gaze was riveted upon that fair flower of royalty. The enunciation was as perfect as the intonation was melodious and I think it is impossible to hear a more excellent utterance than that of the Queen's English, by the English Queen.

Fanny Kemble herself won considerable fame both in England and America for her eloquence and talent in acting. She came from a theatrical family. Her aunt was the famous actress Sarah Siddons.

The 'ideal' maiden, both in looks and morals, was much in evidence in the fiction of the nineteenth century. A delightful example is Rosamund in George Eliot's Middlemarch, *published in 1872:*

Rosamund never showed any unbecoming knowledge, was always that combination of correct sentiments, music, dancing, drawing and elegant note-writing, private album for extracted verse, and perfect blonde loveliness, which made the irresistible woman for the doomed man of that date. Think no unfair evil of her pray; she had no wicked plots, nothing sordid or mercenary; in fact she never thought of money except as something necessary which other people would always provide. She was not in the habit of devising falsehoods, and if her statements were no direct clue to fact, why they were not intended in that light. They were – among her elegant accomplishments – intended to please. She was a rare compound of beauty, cleverness and amiability.

The conventionality of her heroine belies the unconventionality of the life of Mary Ann Evans, the woman behind the pseudonym George Eliot. Recognised in her time as the greatest living English novelist, she lived in London with George Lewes, himself a literary man and a great support to her in her work.

Doris Lessing's picture of a twentieth-century teenager in her book The Children of Violence, *published in 1952, not only brings us up-to-date, but also puts the individual woman into a larger context of time, space and condition:*

Martha was adolescent, and therefore bound to be unhappy; British and therefore uneasy and defensive; in the fourth decade of the twentieth century, and therefore inescapably beset with problems of race and class; female, and obliged to repudiate the shackled women of the past.

Doris Lessing is the daughter of a British Army Captain. She was born in Iran and spent her girlhood in Southern Rhodesia, now Zimbabwe. For nearly forty years she has lived in Britain. Her books, which explore the problems of women's independence, political and moral dilemmas as well as spiritual and mystical themes, have won her worldwide acclaim.

So much is expected of the young, through the ideals and standards set for them. In some instances they are able to reach beyond themselves to amaze and astound us with their achievements. The awareness that Elizabeth Barrett Browning showed, for instance, of her own possibilities at an incredibly early age almost put her beyond childhood. At fourteen (in 1820) she wrote as follows in Glimpses into My Own Life and Literary Character*:*

I was always of a determined and, if thwarted, violent disposition. My actions and temper were infinitely more inflexible at three years old than now at fourteen. At that early age I can perfectly remember reigning in the Nursery and being renowned amongst the servants for self love and excessive passion.

At four and a half my great delight was pouring over fairy phenomenon and the actions of necromancers. At five I supposed myself a heroine.

I perfectly remember the delight I felt when I attained my sixth birthday. I enjoyed my triumph to a great degree over the inhabitants of the Nursery, there being no Upstart to dispute my authority.

At four I first mounted Pegasus, but at six I thought myself privileged to show off feats of horsemanship. In my Sixth year, for some lines on virtue, I received a ten-shilling note enclosed in a letter which was addrest 'to the Poet Laureate of Hope End'. I mention this because I received much more pleasure from the word Poet than from the ten-shilling note. I did not understand the meaning of the word Laureate, but it being explained to me by dearest Mama the idea first presented itself to me of celebrating our Birthdays by my verse. Poet Laureate of Hope End was too great a title to lose.

At seven I began to think of 'forming my taste'. I read the History of England and Rome. At eight I perused the History of Greece . . .

At nine I felt much pleasure from the effusions of my imaginations in the adorned drapery of versifications. The subject of my studies was Pope's *Iliad*, some passages from Shakespeare and novels which I enjoyed to their full extent.

At ten my poetry was entirely formed by the style of written authors and I read that I might write.

At eleven I wished to be considered an authoress. Novels were thrown aside, Poetry and Essays were my studies, and I felt the most ardent desire to understand the learned languages. To comprehend even the Greek alphabet was a delight inexpressible. For eight months during this year I never remember having diverted my attention to any other object than the ambition of gaining fame and never had a better opinion of my own talents. In short I was in infinite danger of being as vain as I was inexperienced. During this dangerous period I was from home and the fever of a heated imagination was perhaps increased by the intoxicating gaieties of a watering place, Ramsgate, where we were then and where I commenced my poem 'The Battle of Marathon' now in print!

At twelve I enjoyed a literary life in all its pleasures. Metaphysics were my highest delight. At this age I was in great danger of becoming the founder of a religion of my own. This year I read Milton for the first time through, together with Shakespeare and Pope's Homer. I had now attained my thirteenth birthday. I perused all modern authors. I read Homer in the original with delight inexpressible together with Virgil.

I am now fourteen and since those days of my tenderest infancy my character has not changed.

A year after writing this, Elizabeth Barrett Browning became a semi-invalid and channelled her energies even more into scholastic pursuits, spending the next ten years learning German, Spanish and Hebrew.

This same kind of appreciation of worth and potential comes

Plate 2 Etching by Gwendoline Raverat, 1930

through in the daily diary written by a young Scottish girl early in the nineteenth century. Marjory Fleming was born on 15 January 1803. In September 1811 she wrote: 'We are surrounded by measles at present on every side.' In November of that year she caught the disease and died from what was then called 'water in the head' – meningitis. Marjory died before her ninth birthday but her diaries, from which I am quoting here, were preserved for posterity. Apart from showing a prodigious literary talent, they demonstrate remarkable perception in their accounts of her girlish aims, and failures, of achieving 'ideal feminine goodness'.

I confess that I have been
more like a little young
Devil then a creature for
when Isabella went up
the stairs to teach me religion and my multi-
plication and to be good
and all my other lessons
I stamped with my feet
and threw my new hat
which she made on the
ground and was sulky an
was dreadfully pasionate
but she never whipped me
but gently said Marjory
go into another room and
think what a great crime
you are committing
letting your temper
git the better of you
but I went so sulkely that
the Devil got the better of me
but she never never whip
me so that I think I would
be the better of it and the
next time that I behave
ill I think she should do it
for she never does it but she
is very indulgent to me but
I am very ungrateful to hir.

To Day I have been very
ungrateful and bad and
disobedient Isabella gave
me my writing I wrote
so ill that she took it
away and locked it up
in her desk where I
stood trying to open
it till she made me come
and read my bible
but
I was in a bad homour
and red it so carelesly
and ill that she took
it from me and her
blood ran cold but she
never punished me
she is as gental as a lamb.
to me an ungrateful girl

Isabella has given me praise
for checking my temper for I
was sulkey when she was
kneeling an hole hour teachin
me to write

I am now going to tell you
about the horrible and wretched
plague that my multiplication
gives me you cant conceive it –
the most Devlish thing is 8 times 8
and 7 times 7 is what nature itselfe
cant endure.

Today I pronounced a
word which should never
come out of a lady's lips it was
that I called John a Impu-
dent Bitch and Isabella afterwards told
me that I should never say
it even in joke but she kindly
forgave me because I said
tha I would not do it again

I will tell you what I think
made me in so bad a homo-
ur is I got 1 or 2 cups of that
bad bad sina tea toDay
Last night I behaved extremely ill and threw my
work in the stairs and
would not pick it up
which was very wrong
indeed

As this is Sunday I must be
gin to write serious thoughts
as Isabella bids me. I am
thinking how I should Improve
the many talents I have.
I am very sory I have
threwn them away it is
shoking to think of it when
many have not half
the instruction I have
because Isabella teaches
me to or three hours every
day in reading and
writing and arethmatick
and many other things
and religion into the bar
gan. On Sunday she
teaches me to be virtuous.

Susanna Burney wrote a letter when she was just fourteen describing her sisters' achievements and failures in the 1760s. Again we see a remarkable maturity as she compares her sisters Hetty and Fanny, the latter destined to become one of the most brilliant writers of her time.

Hetty seems a good deal more lively than she used to appear at Paris; whether it is that her spirits are better, or that the great liveliness of the inhabitants made her appear grave there by comparison, I know not: but she was there remarkable for being *serieuse*, and is here for being gay and lively. She is a most sweet girl. My sister Fanny is unlike her in almost everything, yet both are very amiable, and love each other as sincerely as ever sisters did. The characteristics of Hetty seem to be wit, generosity, and openness of heart; Fanny's – sense, sensibility and bashfulness and even a degree of prudery. Her understanding is superior, but her diffidence gives her a bashfulness before company with whom she is not intimate, which is a disadvantage to her. My eldest sister shines in conversation, because, though modest, she is totally free from any *mauvaise honte*; were Fanny equally so, I am persuaded she would shine no less. I am afraid that my eldest sister is too communicative, and that my sister Fanny is too reserved. They are both charming girls.

The 'too reserved' Fanny published her first novel Evelina *or* The History of a Young Lady's Entry into the World *in 1778 unaided and anonymously. It won for her immediate fame and entry into the highest literary circles of her age. It was Fanny, too, who led a full and adventurous life and recorded it with brilliance and wit in* The Diary and Letters of Madame D'Arblay, *published soon after her death in 1840.*

Jane Austen is another of our great writers whose early literary efforts show maturity of thought and perception and a characteristic irony. This extract is from Love and Friendship, *a novel in a series of letters written in 1795 before Jane was fifteen years old. It is the fourth letter from Laura to Marianne:*

Our neighbourhood was small, for it consisted only of your mother. She may probably have already told you that being left by her Parents in indigent Circumstances she had retired into Wales on economical motives. There it was, our friendship first commenced. Isabel was then one and twenty – Tho' pleasing both in her Person and Manners (between ourselves) she never possessed the hundredth part of my beauty or Accomplishments. Isabel had seen the World. She had passed 2 Years at one of the first Boarding schools in London; had spent a fortnight in Bath & had supped one night in Southampton.

'Beware my Laura (she would often say) Beware of the insipid Vanities and idle Dissipations of the Metropolis of England; Beware of the unmeaning Luxuries of Bath & of the Stinking fish of Southampton.' 'Alas (exclaimed I) how am I to avoid those evils I shall never be exposed to? What probability is there of my ever tasting the Dissipations of London, the Luxuries of Bath or the stinking Fish of Southampton? I who am doomed to waste my Days of Youth & Beauty in an humble Cottage in the Vale of Uske.'

Ah! little did I then think I was ordained so soon to quit that humble Cottage for the Deceitfull Pleasures of the World.

adieu
Laura

Jane Austen was the youngest of seven children of the Rector of the country parish of Steventon in Hampshire. She received a thorough education, privately at home and also at schools in Oxford, Southampton and Reading. In 1801 she moved to Bath with her family. After her father's death in 1805 she lived with her mother and sister in Southampton. Then from 1809 she lived with her brother in Chawton, Hampshire until her death in 1817. During her lifetime her works were published anonymously and brought her little fame and very little money.

Harriet Martineau provides us with an image of great resolution and determination at an early age when she came to terms with deafness. From her autobiography we read of her feelings at the onset of her impairment at the age of fourteen (in 1816):

My deafness when new was the uppermost thing in my mind day and night . . . I was young enough for vows, was, indeed, at the very age of vows – and I made a vow of patience about this infirmity – that I would smile in every moment of anguish from it, and that I would never lose temper at any consequences from it – from losing public worship [then the greatest conceivable privation] to the spoiling of my cap borders by the use of the trumpet I forsaw I must arrive at . . . With such a temper as mine was then, an affliction so worrying, so unintermitting, so mortifying, so isolating as loss of hearing must 'Kill or cure' . . . but it took a long time to effect the cure, and it was so far from being evident or even at all perceptible when I was fifteen, that my parents were determined by medical advice, to send me from home.

Harriet Martineau's resolve sprang largely from the unsympathetic attitudes of her family who, frequently within her

Plate 3 'She's tam'd and tortur'd into
foreign graces, to sport
her pretty face in public places'.
Etching by Maria Cosway, 1800

hearing, would say such things as: 'We'll be as hoarse as ravens or worn-out completely before long.' Despite her disability, she achieved considerable respect as a novelist and journalist.

The Brontë sisters are a fine example of triumph over circumstances. Their rigorous upbringing, misfortunes and family sorrows are portrayed in the novels and poetry familiar to us, which are among the finest in English literature. Perhaps their greatest achievement was that they produced such richness in their writings from the limitations of their experience. They were brought up in the vicarage of Haworth on the edge of the Yorkshire moors by an aunt who hated living in the north of England and a father who retreated into alcoholism as the years went by. Their mother had died when they were still very young. We have a glimpse of that restricted background in the diary that Emily and Anne wrote together. This extract was written in 1834 when they were respectively fourteen and sixteen years old:

Diary of Emily Jane Brontë and Anne Brontë – November 24th 1834, Monday.

I fed Rainbow, Diamond, Snowflake and Jaspar this morning – Branwell went down to Mr Driver's and brought news that Sir Robert Peel was going to be invited to stand for Leeds. Anne and I have been peeling apples for Charlotte to make us an apple pudding and for aunt, nuts and apples . . . Charlotte said she made puddings perfectly and she was of a quick but limited intellect . . . aunt has come into the kitchen just now and said – 'where are your feet Anne?' – Anne answered, 'on the floor, aunt'. Papa opened the parlour door and gave Branwell a letter saying 'Here Branwell read this and then show it to your aunt and Charlotte'. The Gondales are discovering the interior of Gaaldine. Sally Mosley is washing in the back kitchen (end of first side).

2nd side – It is past twelve o'clock Anne and I have not tidied ourselves done our bed work or done our lessons and we want to go out and play. We are going to have for dinner Boiled Beef, Turnips, potatoes and apple pudding. The kitchen is in a very untidy state. Anne and I have not done our music exercise which consists of b major. Tabby said on my putting my pen in her face 'Ya, – pitter pottering there instead of pilling a potate. I answered, 'O dear, O dear, O dear, I will directly' – with that I get up, take a knife and begin pilling (finished pilling the potatoes) Papa going to walk. Mr Sunderland expected. Anne said 'I say, I wonder what we shall be like and where we shall be – if all goes on well in the year 1874 – in which year I shall be in my 57th year, Anne going in her 55th year, Branwell will be going in his 58th year and Charlotte in her 59th year, hoping we shall all be well at that time, we close our paper.

Emily and Anne
November the 24th 1834

The Brontë children were left much to their own devices, playing among themselves, reading and inventing their own plays. Among their favourite books were The Arabian Nights, *Aesop's fables,* The Pilgrim's Progress, *the Bible, Homer and other serious books.*

The dreams and fantasies, so much a part of that childhood, made their literary achievements possible. Even when she had left the Haworth parsonage home, Charlotte still felt imprisoned by her environment, her only escape being the 'land of thought'. The first part of this extract is from a letter Charlotte wrote to Ellen Nussey in July 1835; it is followed by a fragment written in 1836 when she had been teaching at Roe Head for one year.

We are all about to divide, Break up, separate. Emily is going to school, Branwell is going to London and I am going to be a governess. This last determination I formed myself, knowing I should have to take the step sometime . . . and knowing also that papa would have enough to do with his limited income should Branwell be placed at the R.A. and Emily go to Roe Head. I am going to teach in the very school where I myself was taught . . . and, in truth, since I must enter a situation my Lines have fallen in pleasant places. I both love and respect Miss Wooler.

All this day I have been in a dream, half miserable and half ecstatic – miserable because I could not follow it out uninterruptedly, and ecstatic because it showed almost in the vivid light of reality the ongoings of the infernal world. I had been toiling for nearly an hour with Miss Lister, Miss Marriott and

Ellen Cook, striving to teach them the distinction between an article and a substansive. The parsing lesson was completed, a dead silence had succeeded it in the school room and I sat sinking from irritation and weariness into a kind of lethargy. The thought came over me, am I to spend all the best part of my life in this wretched bondage forcibly suppressing my rage at the idleness, the apathy and the hyperbolical and most asinine stupidity of those fat-headed oafs and on compulsion assuming an air of kindness, patience, and assiduity? Must I from day to day sit chained to this chair prisoned within these four bare walls, while these glorious summer suns are burning in heaven and the year is revolving in its richest glow and declaring at the close of every summer's day the time I am losing, will never come again? Stung to the heart with this reflection I started up and mechanically walked to the window – a sweet August morning was smiling without . . . I shut the window and went back to my seat. Then came on me, rushing impetuously all the mighty phantasm that we conjured from nothing to a system strong as some religious creed. I felt as if I could have written gloriously – I longed to write . . . If I had had time to indulge it I felt that the vague sensations of that moment would have settled down into some narrative better at least than anything I have ever produced before. But just then a Dolt came up with a lesson. I thought I should have vomited . . .

I am just going to write because I cannot help it. A. Cook on one side of me, E. Lister on the other and Miss Wooler in the background, stupidity the atmosphere, school books the employment, asses the society. What in all this is there to remind me of the divine, silent, unseen land of thought, dim now and indefinite as the dream of a dream, the shadow of a shade.

This magic side of childhood, this ability to transcend reality through imagination, has produced some splendid literary illustrations for us. Mary Shelley, daughter of Mary Wollstonecraft and the philosopher William Godwin, describes this state as forming 'castles in the air':

As a child I scribbled. Still I had a dearer pleasure than this, which was the formation of castles in the air – the indulging in waking dreams, the following up trains of thought, which had for their subject the formation of a succession of imaginary incidents. My dreams were at once more fantastic and agreeable than my writings. In the latter I was a close imitator, but my dreams were all my own. I accounted for them to nobody, they were my refuge when annoyed, my dearest pleasure when free.

The most famous product of Mary Shelley's imagination was Frankenstein, *written in 1816 while staying in Switzerland with her husband Percy Bysshe Shelley. It arose from a suggestion by Lord Byron that the Shelleys should each write a ghost story during their visit. The extract I have quoted above is taken from the preface to the third edition of* Frankenstein, *published in 1818.*

Dame Edith Evans, when she was very young, acted her fantasies, as many children do. In the biography of this great British actress, written by Bryan Forbes, Dame Edith is quoted talking about her early years:

'When I was a little girl I used to pretend to be people. I used to say, to myself of course, "Now I'm being Dolly Turtle" or what-ever-her-name-was, walking down the stairs. Nobody saw me, nobody, but I used to enjoy being somebody else. I never wanted to be me.'

Answering the question 'Did you know from the start you'd become an actress?' Dame Edith Evans gave this surprising reply:

'I never played with a toy theatre, I never collected stage autographs, in fact I was not in the least bit stage struck or interested in the theatre at all. There weren't any beginnings. The only thing I remember saying when I was asked what I wanted to be was, I think, a rather significant one. I said: "I don't want a job that I can see the end of." That is a very ungrammatical sentence, but I was never very good at grammar. I'm pretty sure that is how I phrased it and that little maxim more or less stayed with me all my life.'

Little did Dame Edith Evans know as a young girl that she would become one of the greatest exponents of Shakespeare and take part in many major productions on stage and screen.

The fantasies of childhood can easily turn into fears. This extract from Edna O'Brien's A Pagan Place, *published in 1971, graphically describes the kind of fears that creep into the minds of many young children at one time or another:*

After she'd done her day's work you sat on her lap. You put your ear to the wall of her stomach and you could hear her insides glugging away. Your father told you to get down out of there, to get down. Put his hand under her chin and forced her face up, told her to smile, smile, told her she was getting old, told her she had wrinkles, called her Mud, short for mother. She had to go across the landing to his room. As edict.

The landing was big and cold. There was a sofa that never got sat on and a fringed mat that hardly ever got shook out. There was an embroidered picture that said 'There's a rose in the heart of New York'. A funny thing to say. You saw New York on a postcard and it was all skyscrapers.

You were frightened of lockjaw and also of being kidnapped. In your mother you were safe and that was the only time you couldn't get kidnapped and that was the nearest you ever were to any other human being. Between you and your mother there was only a membrane, wafer thin. Being near someone on the inside was not the same thing as being near them on the outside, even though the latter could involve hugging and kissing.

Once you were one with her. She didn't like it. She told the woman with the hair like Mrs Simpson how she was sick and bilious all the time. She never kissed you good night, there was no need for that. When you turned to the wall she turned too, put her arms around you, underneath your ribs, clenched you once or twice. You prayed, she prayed, the same prayer.

As I lay me down to sleep
I pray to God my soul to keep
And if I die before I wake
I pray to God my soul to take.

You did not want her to die.

The unknown is a vast source of fear at any age but it is all the greater in childhood because there is so much unknown! The first awareness of sexuality, in oneself or others, when coupled with a certainty that sexual feelings should be suppressed, can cause paralysing fear. In 'Professions for Women' from Virginia Woolf's Collected Essays, *we are given an insight into the influence on her early writings of the repressions and conflicts of her background, and the fears these wrought in her.*

I want you to imagine me writing a novel in a state of trance. I want you to figure to yourselves a girl sitting with a pen in her hand, which for minutes and indeed for hours, she never dips into the inkpot. The image that comes to my mind when I think of this girl is the image of a fisherman lying sunk in dreams on the verge of a deep lake with a rod held out over the ware. She was letting her imagination sweep unchecked round every rock and cranny of the world that lies submerged in the depth of our subconscious being. Now came the experience that I believe to be far commoner with women writers than with men. The line raced through the girl's fingers. Her imagination had rushed away. It had sought the pools, the depths, the dark places where the largest fish slumber. And then there was a smash. There was an explosion. There was foam and confusion. The imagination had dashed itself against something hard. The girl was roused from her dream. To speak without figure she had thought of something about the body, about the passions, which it was unfitting for her as a woman to say. Men, her reason told her, would be shocked. The consciousness of what men will say of a woman who speaks the truth about her passions had roused her from her artist's state of unconsciousness. She could write no more.

Katherine Mansfield was born in New Zealand in the days of the British Empire. She lived a great part of her short life in England following a literary career and earning a wide reputation as an original and experimental writer. In her short story 'Her First Ball', Katherine Mansfield stirs memories of excitement, nervousness and expectancy as she describes a young lady about to take a big step into the grown-up world:

The dancing had not begun yet, but the band had stopped tuning and the noise was so great it seemed that when it did begin to play it would never be heard. Leila, pressing close to Meg, looking over Meg's shoulder, felt that even the little quivering coloured flags strung across the ceiling were talking.

She quite forgot to be shy, she forgot how in the middle of dressing she had sat down on the bed with one shoe off and one shoe on and begged her mother to ring up her cousins and say she couldn't go after all. She clutched her fan and gazing at the gleaming, golden floor, the azaleas, the lanterns, the stage at one end with its red carpet and gilt chairs and the band in a corner, she thought breathlessly, 'How heavenly, how simply heavenly'.

The band began playing, a great wave of music came flying over the gleaming floor, breaking the groups up into couples, scattering them, sending them spinning.

Leila had learned to dance at boarding school. Every Saturday afternoon the Boarders were hurried off to a little corrugated iron mission hall, where Miss Eccles (of London) held her 'Select' classes. But the difference between the dusty smelling hall – with calico texts on the walls, the poor terrified little woman in a velvet toque, with rabbit's ears, thumping the cold piano, Miss Eccles poking the girls' feet with a long white wand – and this was so tremendous that Leila was sure if her partner didn't come, and she had to listen to that marvellous music and to watch the others sliding, gliding over the golden floor, she would die at least, or faint, or lift her arms and fly out of one of those dark windows that showed the stars.

2

In love, marriage and motherhood

Womanhood does not leave behind the little girl we have seen in those earlier passages. In the innocence and dreams that survive, she stays and is remembered. Now, as she goes out to meet the world and test its opportunities, we are treated to a new pageant of images showing woman as Dryden described her – 'a various and changeful thing'.

Nature has set the mould into which woman is expected to fit, and society has placed her within a family structure to fulfil her role of wife and mother. So it has been for centuries: only the terms and conditions have changed. In the passages I am offering here we see how woman accepts or rejects her role, or reaches a compromise. We see her in love, contemplating love, losing love, feeling passion and forging friendships. In marriage we see her happy and hopeful, serene and secure, frustrated and bitter, fettered and fretful. In motherhood she radiates joy, burns with resentment.

First, to love. Uniquely experienced by each one of us, it defies definition. Woman's perspective of love produces some poignantly expressive writing as she tries to pin down its concept, describe its ecstasy and passion, cope with its frustrations, mourn its loss. Dame Iris Murdoch, distinguished British novelist and philosopher, presents her concept of love in The Sovereignty of Good, *published in 1970:*

I think that Good and Love should not be identified, and not only because human love is usually self-assertive. The concepts, even when the idea of love is purified, still play different roles. Good is the magnetic centre towards which love naturally moves . . . When true good is loved, even impurely or by

Plate 4 'Girl Leaning on a Gate' by Lady Edna Clarke-Hall

accident, the quality of the love is automatically refined, and when the soul is turned towards Good the highest part of the soul is enlivened. Love is the tension between the imperfect soul and the magnetic perfection which is conceived of as beyond it. And when we try perfectly to love what is imperfect our love goes to its object VIA Good to be thus purified and made unselfish and just. The mother loving the retarded child or loving the tiresome elderly relation. Love is the general name of the quality of attachment and it is capable of infinite degradation and is the source of our greatest errors; but when it is even partially refined it is the energy and passion of the soul in its search for Good, the force that joins us to Good and joins us to the world through Good. Its existence is the unmistakable sign that we are spiritual creatures, attracted by excellence and made for the Good. It is a reflection of the warmth and light of the sun.

Anne Finch published her 'Essay on Marriage' in 1946. In this section chosen from her much longer poem, she is asking us to redefine love and to examine what we might be expecting from it:

O, love, in your sweet name enough
Illusory pretentious stuff
Is talked and written. Myth and dream
Fix the contemporary scheme
In alien shapes. Can we not make
Some simple statement which will shake
Our valued preconceptions loose;
And, putting to a better use
The innocent and candid sense
Of everyday experience,
Build up a picture of known fact
More subtle, brilliant, and exact?

Tradition is no guide. The old
Romantic impulse has gone cold;
The Christian ethic has in fact
Small bearing on the way we act;
And the inevitable urge
To let a newer style emerge
(Masked by adherence to some creed

We can't believe in, and don't need)
Appears, sporadic and abrupt,
As something formless and corrupt,
Conflicting with the other drives
And broader movement of our lives;
While still an individual past
Weighs on us too, and breeds the last
Infirmity of intellect –
We must achieve what we expect.

Love is not always immediately recognisable, as novelist Katherine Mansfield discusses in Love and Mushrooms, *written in 1917:*

If only one could tell true love from false love as one can tell mushrooms from toadstools. With mushrooms it is so simple – you salt them well, put them aside and have patience. But with love, you have no sooner lighted on anything that bears even the remotest resemblance to it than you are perfectly certain it is not only a genuine specimen, but perhaps THE only genuine mushroom ungathered. It takes a dreadful number of toadstools to make you realise that life is not one big mushroom.

Katherine Mansfield's journals and letters were edited by her second husband, John Middleton Murry, and published after her death from tuberculosis in a French sanatorium in 1923 at the age of thirty-five. She left her first husband after only a few days. On the relationships between lovers she wrote:

We are neither male nor female. We are a compound of both. I choose the male who will develop and expand the male in me; he chooses me to expand the female in him. Being made 'whole'. Yes, but that's a process. By love serve ye one another . . . And why I choose ONE man for this rather than many is for safety. We bind ourselves within a ring and that ring is as it were a wall against the outside world. It is our refuge, our shelter. Here the tricks of life will not be played. Here is SAFETY for us to grow.

In her poem 'Amo Ergo Sum' Kathleen Raine pronounces the vibrant influences of woman's love, love which reaches beyond the personally passionate to encompass all forms of nature and the living world. This poem is one of the collection of poems by Kathleen Raine entitled The Year One, *published in 1952.*

Because I love
  The sun pours out its rays of living gold
  Pours out its gold and silver on the sea.

Because I love
  The earth upon her astral spindle winds
  Her ecstasy-producing dance.

Because I love
  Clouds travel on the winds through wide skies
  Skies wide and beautiful, blue and deep.

Because I love
  Wind blows white sails,
  The wind blows over flowers, the sweet wind blows.

Because I love
  The ferns grow green, and green the grass, and green
  The transparent sunlit trees.

Because I love
  Larks rise up from the grass
  And all the leaves are full of singing birds.

Because I love
  The summer air quivers with a thousand wings,
  Myriads of jewelled eyes burn in the light.

Because I love
  The iridescent shells upon the sand
  Take forms as fine and intricate as thought.

Because I love
  There is an invisible way across the sky,
  Birds travel by that way, the sun and moon
  And all the stars travel that path by night.

Because I love
  There is a river flowing all night long.

Because I love
  All night the river flows into my sleep,
  Ten thousand living things are sleeping in my arms,
  And sleeping wake, and flowing are at rest.

The mystical quality of Kathleen Raine's poem is also characteristic of Christina Rossetti's love poetry. Although her experience was derived from an ill-fated love life and she remained single and in constant poor health until her death in 1894 at the age of sixty, the following poem radiates the universal joy love brings.

A Birthday

My heart is like a singing bird
  Whose nest is in a watered shoot;
My heart is like an apple tree
  Whose boughs are bent with thickset fruit;
My heart is like a rainbow shell
  That paddles in a halcyon sea;
My heart is gladder than all these
  Because my love is come to me.

Raise me a dais of silk and down;
  Hang it with vair and purple dyes;
Carve it in doves and pomegranates,
  And peacocks with a hundred eyes;
Work it in gold and silver grapes,
  In leaves and silver fleur-de-lys;
Because the Birthday of my life
  Is come, my love is come to me.

The expression of woman's love and passion which comes through so strongly in these poems has not always been acceptable in society. A great part of woman's struggle for emancipation in the twentieth century has been for the recognition and the accommodation of the amorous part of her nature.

There have always been some who have fearlessly revealed their true natures. Mary Wollstonecraft was one. Her own ideas and practice of free love were far ahead of her time. In 1794 she wrote to her former lover, American writer Gilbert Imlay, by whom she had a child:

Love is a want of my heart. I have examined myself lately with more care than formerly, and find, that to deaden is not to calm the mind. Aiming at tranquility, I have almost destroyed all the energy of my soul . . . Despair, since the birth of my child, has rendered me stupid . . . the desire of regaining peace (do you understand me?) has made me forget the respect due to my own emotions – sacred emotions that are the sure harbingers of the delights I was formed to enjoy – and shall enjoy, for nothing can extinguish the heavenly spark.

Charlotte Brontë expressed the same intensity of feeling in her fiction. This passage is taken from Jane Eyre, *published in 1847. Jane Eyre is a young woman employed as a governess. She falls in love with her employer, Mr Rochester. Her love survives many romantic vicissitudes and finally reaches marital consummation. Here Jane is speaking her mind, believing Rochester to be on the point of marrying Blanche Ingram.*

The vehemence of emotion, stirred by grief and love within me, was claiming master and struggling for full sway, asserting a right to predominate, to overcome, to live, rise and reign at last; yes, and to speak.

'I grieve to leave Thornfield . . . I love it, because I have lived in it a full and delightful life – momentarily at least. I have not been trampled on, I have not been petrified, I have not been buried with inferior minds, and excluded from every glimpse of communion with what I reverence, with what I delight in – with an original, a vigorous and expanded mind. I have known you, Mr Rochester; and it strikes me with terror and anguish to feel I absolutely must be torn from you for ever. I see the necessity of departure; and it is like looking at the necessity of death.

'I tell you I must go! Do you think that I can stay to become nothing to you? Do you think I am an automaton? a machine without feelings? and can bear to have my morsel of bread snatched from my lips, and my drop of living water dashed from my cup? Do you think, because I am poor, obscure, plain and little, I am soulless and heartless? You think wrong – I have as much soul as you – and full as much heart! And if God had gifted me with some beauty and much wealth, I should have made it as hard for you to leave me as it is now for me to leave you. I am not talking to you now through the medium of custom, conventionalities nor even of mortal flesh: it is my spirit that addresses your spirit; just as if both had passed through the grave, and we stood at God's feet, as we are!'

Aphra Behn's poem gives us an explicit description of woman's eroticism. It may surprise sexually liberated women of today that it was written three hundred years ago.

The Dream

All trembling in my arms Aminta lay,
Dafending of the bliss I strove to take;
Raising my rapture by her kind delay,
Her force so charming was and weak.
The soft resistance did betray the grant,
While I pressed on the heaven of my desires;
Her rising breasts with nimbler motions pant;
Her dying eyes assume new fires.
Now to the height of languishment she grows,
And still her looks new charms put on;
Now the last mystery of Love she knows,
We sigh, and kiss: I waked, and all was done.

'Twas but a dream, yet by my heart I knew,
Which still was panting, part of it was true:
Oh how I strove the rest to have believed;
Ashamed and angry to be undeceived!

Jean Rhys's first love affair was 'a dream come true'. She reminisces about it in her unfinished autobiography Smile Please, *first published in 1979. She writes about her time as a young actress just prior to the First World War.*

When my first love affair came to an end I wrote this poem:
I didn't know
I didn't know
I didn't know
Then I settled down to be miserable.

But it still annoys me when my first object of worship is supposed to be a villain. Or perhaps the idea at the back of this is that his class was oppressing mine. He had money, I had none.

On the contrary. I realise now what a very kind man he must have been. I was an ignorant girl, a shy girl. And when I read novels describing present-day love-making I realise I was also a passive, dull girl. Though I couldn't control my hammering heart when he touched me, I was too shy to say 'I love you'. It would be too much, too important. I couldn't claim so much.

When I first met this man I rather disliked him, and why I came to worship him I don't quite know. I loved his voice, the way he walked. He was like all the men in the books I had ever read about London. He lived in Berkeley Square and I got used to the warmth of the fires all over the house, the space, the comforts. When I left to go back to my rather cold room I was never envious . . . He was a dream come true for me, and one doesn't question dreams or envy them.

Confusion, doubt and misunderstanding seem a recurring feature of woman's experience of love. In so many cases it is just plain and simple ignorance that is the problem. Dame Ellen Terry wrote to George Bernard Shaw in 1896:

Of course, there's kissing and kissing. I'm a very kissing person. But some girls kiss 'in conservatories' (Oh, don't you know what I mean – the dancer they have met an hour ago, the next one probably and the next – ad lib). I never could have done that. Very many women kiss two men at the same time. Pigs! I'll never forget my first kiss. I made myself such a donkey over it, and always laugh now when I remember. Mr Watts kissed me in the Studio one day, but sweetly and gently, all tenderness and kindness, and then I was what they call 'engaged' to him and all the rest of it, and my people hated it, and I was in Heaven for I knew I was to live with those pictures. 'Always' – I thought, and to sit to that gentle Mr Watts and clean his brushes, and play my idiotic piano to him, and sit with him there in wonderland (the Studio). Then I got ill and had to stay at Holland House – and then – he kissed me – DIFFERENTLY – not much differently but a little, and I told no one for a fortnight, but when I was alone with Mother . . . I told her I MUST be married to him NOW because I was going to have a baby!!! and she believed me!! Oh, I tell you I thought I knew everything then . . . I was SURE THAT KISS MEANT GIVING ME A BABY!

Such naivety may seem harmless and amusing on the face of it, and it was certainly commonplace. Ellen Terry married the painter G F Watts who was twenty-seven years her senior, but their marriage broke up after ten months. She returned to the stage to a brilliant career as an actress and later a theatre manager. She was married three times but never successfully.

Frustration and rejection have often prompted women to express the depth of their passion. Aphra Behn's obsession with the 'Dark Gentleman' inspired some of her most intimate and moving poetry and letters, such as this one written during their relationship which lasted until her death in 1689. The 'Dark Gentleman' was probably John Doyle, a man of sophistication, wit and intelligence who did not reciprocate Aphra Behn's feelings. He is thought to have been homosexual and, although he was a Gray's Inn lawyer, he was a ne'er-do-well.

You would not be in love for all the world, yet wish I were so. Possibly you will wonder what compels me to write; what moves me to send where I find so little welcome; nay, where I meet with such returns; it may be that I wonder too. Was that, my friend, was that the esteem you profess? Who grows cold first? Who is changed? and who is the aggressor? 'Tis I was first in friendship and shall be last in constancy. I grow desperate fond of you, and would fain be used well; if not I will march off. Do not shame me with your perpetual ill opinion. Witnessing your passing by the end of the street where I live, and squandering away your time at any coffee house, rather than allow me what you know in your soul is the greatest blessing of my life, your dear dull melancholy company.

You left me to torments. You went to love, alone, and left me love and rage, fevers and calentures, even madness itself. Indeed, indeed my soul, I know not to what degree I love you; let it suffice I do most passionately, and can have no thought of any other man whilst I have life. No! Reproach me, defame me, lampoon me, curse me and kill me when I do. Farewell, I love you more and more every moment of my life.

The 'Problem Pages' of our magazines and newspapers today are still receiving letters like this one, reprinted from a 1693 edition of The Athenian Mercury*:*

When we are in love, and the man won't or can't understand our signs and omens, what in modesty can we do more to open their eyes?

The answer given was:

Alas, poor lady, your case is very hard. Why pull 'em by the nose. Write to 'em or if neither of these will do (as you have been formerly advised) show 'em this question and answer in *The Athenian Mercury.*

To some the release from passion comes as a relief:

I think that the exhilaration of falling out of love is not sufficiently extolled. The escape from the atmosphere of a stuffy room into the fresh night air, with the sky as the limit. The feeling of freedom, of integrity, of being a blissfully unimportant item in an impersonal world, where vicissitudes are not worth a tear. The feeling of being a queen in your own right. It is a true rebirth.

So wrote Stella Bowen in Drawn from Life, *published in 1941. She was married to the author, editor and publisher, Ford Madox Ford.*

In a letter to Fanny Knight in 1817, Jane Austen recommends marriage as an alternative to what was so often the poverty of the spinster:

Single women have a dreadful propensity for being poor – which is one very strong argument in favour of Matrimony. But I need not dwell on such arguments with you, pretty Dear, you do not want inclination. Well, I shall say, as I have often said before, do not be in a hurry. Depend on it, the right man will come at last; you will, in the course of the next two or three years meet with somebody who will so completely attach you that you will feel you never really loved before. And then, by not beginning the business of mothering quite so early in life you will be young in Constitution, Spirits, Figure, and Countenance.

Jane Austen never married, although she had a number of suitors, one of whom she accepted only to reject the following morning.

Mrs Gaskell, writing in the nineteenth century, shows how crucial marriage could be as a source of security in this conver-

sation between Dr Gibson and the pretty widow, Mrs Kirkpatrick, paid companion, in the book Wives and Daughters*:*

Is he going to offer? thought she with a sudden palpitation and a conviction of her willingness to accept a man whom an hour before she had simply looked upon as one of the category of unmarried men to whom marriage was possible. He was only going to make one or two medical inquiries; she found that out very speedily and considered the conversation as rather flat . . .

'It's very stormy weather,' said he.

'Yes, very. My daughter writes me word that for two days last week the packet boat could not sail from Boulogne.'

'Miss Kirkpatrick is at Boulogne, is she?'

'Yes, poor girl . . . A young daughter is a great charge, Mr Gibson, especially when there is only one parent to look after her.'

'You are quite right,' said he, recalled to the remembrance of Molly.

'You are thinking of your own daughter. Dear child. How I should like to see her.'

'I hope you will. I should like you to see her. I should like you to love her as your own.' He swallowed something that rose in his throat, and was nearly choking him.

'Is he going to offer?' she wondered, and she began to tremble in the suspense before he next spoke.

'Could you love her as your daughter – will you try? Will you give me the right of introducing you to her as her future mother, as my wife?'

There! He had done it – whether it was wise or foolish – he had done it; but he was aware that the question as to its wisdom came into his mind the instant that the words were said past recall.

She hid her face in her hands.

'Oh, Mr Gibson,' she said, and then, a little to his surprise and a great deal to her own, she burst into hysterical tears; it was such a wonderful relief to feel that she need not struggle any more for a livelihood.

Mrs Gaskell enjoyed a married life of 'calm and perfect harmony'. She was a very attractive woman and succeeded in writing fiction, articles and autobiographical novels as well as her highly acclaimed biography of Charlotte Brontë.

An escape from her penniless condition was the basis of the proposal which Frances Milton received from Thomas Anthony Trollope in 1808. In reply she unselfishly points out the disadvantage to him of making a hasty union between them:

'It does not require three weeks' consideration, Mr Trollope, to enable me to tell you that the letter you left me with last night was most flattering and gratifying to me. I value your good opinion too highly not to feel that the generous proof you have given me of it must for ever, and in any event, be remembered by me with pride and gratitude. But I fear you are not sufficiently aware that your choice, so flattering to me, is for yourself a very imprudent one . . . in an affair of this kind I do not think it a disadvantage to either party that some time should elapse between the first contemplation and final decision of it. It gives each an opportunity of becoming acquainted with the other's opinion on many important points, which could not be canvassed before it was thought of, and which it would be useless to discuss after it was settled.'

In eventually accepting his offer, Frances Milton exposed herself to an even greater poverty when her husband failed as both lawyer and farmer and she had to raise a large family. She was fifty years old when she wrote the first of over forty books which at last brought her wealth – and fame – and she lived to see the start of her son Anthony Trollope's great literary career.

Jean Rhys, in her unfinished autobiography published in 1979, perceived a deeper meaning to the 'whole business of money and sex':

It seems to me now that the whole business of money and sex is mixed up with something very primitive and deep. When you take money from someone you love it becomes not money but a symbol. The bond is now there. The bond has been established. I am sure the woman's deep-down feeling is 'I belong to this man. I want to belong to him completely.' It is at once humiliating and exciting.

Rhoda Broughton, a nineteenth-century novelist, was the daughter of a clergyman. She remained a spinster and lived and worked with her widowed sister in Oxford. Here she offers us her perception of how a girl felt as a piece of property in 1867. Heroine Nell speaks of the rich, old and ugly Sir Hugh to whom she has been married:

His arm is around my waist and he is brushing my eyes and cheeks and brow with his somewhat bristly moustache, as often as he feels inclined – for am I not his property? Has he not every right to kiss my face off if he chooses – to clasp me and hold me and drag me about in whatever manner he will, for has he not bought me? For a pair of first-class blue eyes warranted fast colour, for ditto superfine red lips, for so many pounds of prime white flesh, he has paid a handsome price on the nail, without any haggling, and now if he may not test the worth of his purchases, poor man, he is hardly used.

All Sir Hugh's other servants, if they dislike their situation, or get tired of them, might give warning and leave; but I, however wearied I might get of mine, could never give warning, could never leave. I am a fixture for life – or a very bad wicked woman.

Money again was the basis of this relationship.

Lady Dalkieth was left a rich widow at the age of thirty-three. Her fortune soon attracted a second husband, Charles Townsend, eight years her junior. Lady Mary Montague, her sister, was appalled by the liaison and prophesied nothing but disaster in a letter she wrote to her daughter in 1750:

I pity poor Lady Dalkieth who, perhaps, thinks herself at present an object of envy; she will be soon undeceived; no rich widow can marry on prudential motives; and where passion is only on one side, every marriage must be miserable. If she thought justly, she would know that no man was ever in love with a woman of forty since the deluge . . . All she can hope for is a cold complaisance, founded on gratitude which is the most uncertain of all foundations for a lasting union. Lady Dalkieth had fond parents and, as I have heard, an obliging husband. Her sorrowful hours are now coming on; they will be new to her, and 'tis a cruel addition to reflect (as she must do) that they have been her own purchasings.

It would be naive to imagine that all marriage proposals are prompted by ardent love.

An irregular proposition of marriage is one of the many colourful incidents in Fanny Burney's diary, which chronicled her life at court. This entry was written in 1788 when she was Second Keeper of the Robes to Queen Charlotte at Kew Palace. Mrs Schwellenburg was a tyrannical, uncouth, ill-tempered but important member of the court.

At length, however, Mrs Schwellenburg broke out into one inquiry which if favourably answered might have appeased all, but truth was too strongly in the way.

'Colonel Goldsworthy always sleeps with me. Sleeps he with you the same?'

In the midst of all my irksome discomfort it was with difficulty I could keep my countenance at this question, which I was forced to negative.

The next evening she repeated it. 'Vell? Sleeps he yet with you? – the Colonel Goldsworthy?'

'Not yet, ma'am,' I hesitatingly answered.

'Oh, very vell! He vill sleep with nobody but me.'

And a little after she added, 'I believe he vill marry you.'

'I believe not, ma'am,' I answered.

And then very gravely she proposed him to me, saying he only wanted a little encouragement, for he was always declaring he wished for a wife, and yet wanted no fortune.

'So for vhat von't you have him?'

I answered we were both perfectly well satisfied apart and equally free from any thoughts of each other.

'Then for vhat,' she cried, 'von't you have Dr Shepherd?'

She is now in the utmost haste to dispose of me! She is an amazing woman. If she asks me any more about the Colonel Goldsworthy and his sleeping, I think I will answer I am too near-sighted to be sure if he is awake or not!

Fanny Burney became thoroughly disenchanted with her position at court and asked permission to retire in 1791. Living in London on a pension, she met the French exile General d'Arblay, whom she married in 1793. After the birth of her son a year later, she took to the pen to support her family.

Mrs Henry Wood, the Victorian novelist, wrote from personal experience of her disappointment in marriage. She was married to an unsympathetic businessman of whom his son wrote: 'he had not a spark of imagination and . . . that it was an effort for him to read a novel'. Mrs Henry Wood wrote in her novel East Lynne, *published in 1895:*

Young lady, when he, who is soon to be your Lord and Master, protests to you that he shall always be as ardent a lover as he is now, believe him if you like, but don't reproach him when disappointment comes . . . It is in the constitution of man, to change, the very essence of his nature . . . his manner must settle down into a calmness, which to you, if you are of an exacting temperament, may look like indifference or coldness, but you will do well to put up with it, for it will never now be otherwise.

A no less pessimistic image of woman in marriage is drawn by Lady Chudleigh in her poem 'To The Ladies', written in 1703:

Wife and Servant are the same,
But only differ in the Name
For when that fatal knot is ty'ed
Which nothing, nothing can divide;
When she the word 'obey' has said,
And Man by Law supreme has made,
Then all that's kind is laid aside,
And nothing left but State and Pride;
Fierce as an Eastern Prince he grow,
And all his innate Rigor show;
Then but to look, to laugh, or speak,
Will the Nuptial Contract break.
Like Mutes she Sights alone must make
And never any Freedom take;
But still be governed by a Nod,
And fear her Husband as her God;
Him still must serve, Him still obey,
And nothing act, and nothing say,
But what her haughty Lord thinks fit.
Who with the Pow'r has the Wit.
Then shun, oh! Shun that wretched State,
And all the fawning Flatterers hate;
Value yourselves, and then despise,
You must be proud, if you'll be wise.

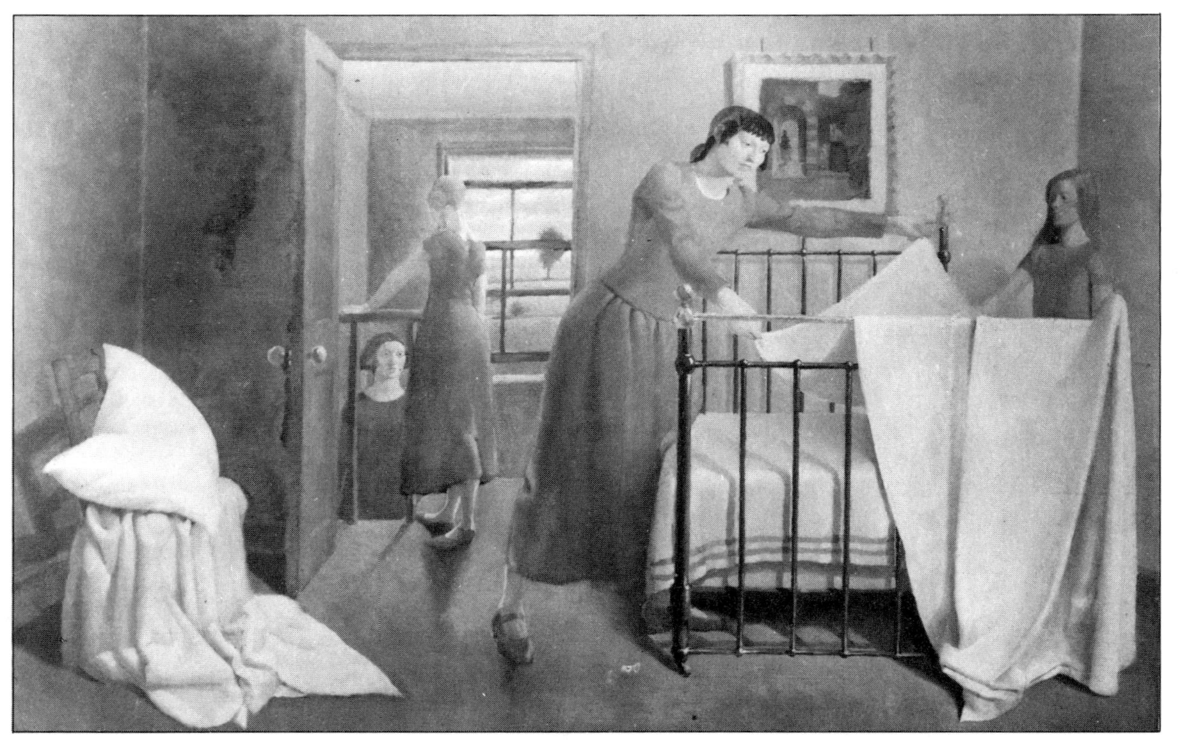

Plate 5 'Any Morning' by Margaret Barker, 1929

Anna Wickham fulfilled herself as wife, mother and poet. She had a deep compassion for less fortunate women as she pictured them so graphically in this poem, published in 1935:

Alas for all the pretty women who marry dull men,
Go into the suburbs and never come out again.
Who lose their pretty faces, and dim their pretty eyes,
Because no one has skill or courage to organise.

What do these pretty women suffer when they marry?
They bear a boy who is like Uncle Harry,
A girl, who is like Aunt Eliza, and new.
These old dull races must breed true.

I would enclose a common in the sun,
And let the young wives out to laugh and run;
I would steal their dull clothes and go away
And leave the pretty naked things to play.

Then I would make a contract with hard Fate
That they see all the men in the world to choose a mate,
And I would summon all the papers in the town
That they dance with Love at a feast, and dance him down.

From the gay unions of choice
We'd have a race of splendid beauty and of thrilling voice,
The world whips frank, gay love with rods,
But frankly, gaily shall we get the gods.

Again from East Lynne, *Mrs Henry Wood gives this heartfelt warning against breaking out of the bonds of marriage which, however tedious, offer security. How often she must have wanted to do so herself despite the fact that her rich husband took her to live on the French Riviera where she fulfilled her life by writing dozens of novels on middle-class English life.*

Lady – wife – mother! Should you ever be tempted to abandon your home, so will you awaken! Whatever trials may be the lot of your married life, though they may magnify themselves to your crushed spirit as beyond the endurance of woman to bear, resolve to bear them; fall down on your knees and pray to be enabled to bear them.

This anonymous Anglo-Saxon elegy, 'The Wife's Complaint', written in the tenth century, is a powerful statement of fierce passions aroused by a wife's estrangement from her husband. In it she recalls their former happiness, curses the author of their separation, and pictures her husband stranded on some distant shore. It is not certain whether this was composed by a woman, but it is thought traditionally possible.

I have wrought these words together out of a wryed existence,
the heart's tally, telling of
the grief I have undergone from girlhood upwards,
old and new, and now more than ever;
for I have never not had some new sorrow,
some fresh affliction to fight against.
The first was my lord's leaving his people here:
crossed crests. To what country I knew not,
wondered where, awoke unhappy.
I left, fared any road, friendless, an outcast,
sought any service to staunch the lack of him.

Then his kinsmen ganged, began to think
thoughts they did not speak, of splitting the wedlock,
so – estranged, alienated – we lived each
alone, a long way apart; how I longed for him!
In his harshness he had brought me here;
and in these parts there were few friendly minded,
worth trusting.

  Trouble in the heart now:
I saw the bitterness, the bound mind
of my matched man, mourning browe,
mirk in his mood, murder in his thoughts.

Our lips had smiled to swear hourly
that nothing should split us – save dying –
nothing else. All that has changed;
it is now as if it never had been,
our friendship. I feel in the wind
That the man dearest to me detests me.
I was banished to this knoll, knotted by woods
to live in a den dug beneath an oak.
Old is this earthen room; it eats at my heart.

I see the thorns up there in thick coverts
on the banks that baulk these black hollows:
not a gay dwelling. Here the grief bred
by lordlack preys on me. Some lovers in this world
live dear to each other, lie warm together
at day's beginning: I go by myself
about these earth caves under the oak tree.
Here I must sit the summer day through,
here weep out the woes of exile,
the hardships heaped upon me. My heart shall never
suddenly sail into slack water,
all the longings of a lifetime unanswered.

May grief and bitterness blast the mind
of that young man! May his mind ache
behind his smiling face! May a flock of sorrows
choke his chest! He would change his tune
if he lived alone in a land of exile
far from his folk.
  Where my friend is stranded
frost crusts the cracked cliff-face,
grey waves grind the shingle.
The mind cannot bear in such a bleak place very much grief.
  He remembers too often
less grim surroundings. Sorrow follows
this too long wait for one who is estranged.

Despite the apparent burdens, marriage and motherhood have generally been preferred to spinsterhood – a word which we don't often use nowadays when we refer to professional women with lifelong careers. The spinster's 'failed femininity' in the past made her a creature to be pitied or at the very least suspected. To follow in her footsteps was the dread of most girls of marriageable age. In her book Daughters and Rebels, *published in 1960, Jessica Mitford describes how such oddities were explained away.*

The Maiden Aunt was often surrounded by an aura of legend, the more mysterious because those of her generation who, like my mother, knew the facts could never be prevailed upon to reveal the full story. The hints that Muv occasionally dropped only deepened the mystery, making it the more disturbing.

'Why didn't she ever marry?' Muv's face would cloud with disapproval at the impertinence of such curiosity about another's private life. 'Well, darling, it's none of your business, but if you must know, something awful happened to her teeth when she was a young girl.' 'What sort of awful thing?' 'I think it's called pyorrhea. Anyway, they started to fall out and for many months she managed to hold them in with bits of bread, but it didn't work . . . now run along, that's all I'm going to tell you.' The horror of it! I could never again look at that particular aunt without visualising a young girl with a glorious Edwardian hairdo, panic-stricken, alone in her room trying to shore up her ruined teeth.

To yet another aunt an even sharper misfortune had occurred. At her first ball, a young man had stepped on her foot. She was laid up for some time, and by the time she recovered it was too late for marriage. 'Can't a person get married even though toothless and footless?' I asked Muv, but she merely frowned and changed the subject.

Dorothy Wordsworth epitomises the devoted sister. She remained unmarried and spent her life housekeeping for her brother William, the poet, and supporting him in his literary career. Her journal and poetry show her great talent in describing the beauties of nature in the Lake District where they lived for fifty years. In her journal she relates an event which, for her, was traumatic:

On Monday, 4th October, 1802, my brother William was married to Mary Hutchinson. I slept a good deal of the night, and rose fresh and well in the morning. At a little after 8 o'clock I saw them go down the avenue towards the church. William had parted from me upstairs. When they were absent my dear little Sara prepared the breakfast. I kept myself quiet as I could but when I saw the two men running up the walk, coming to tell us it was over, I could stand it no longer, and threw myself on the bed, where I lay in stillness, neither hearing or seeing anything till Sara came upstairs to me and said, 'They are coming'. This forced me from the bed where I lay, and I moved, I knew not how, straight forward, faster than my strength could carry me, till I met beloved William, and fell upon his bosom. He and John Hutchinson led me to the house.

It took one of history's greatest Queens to make a virtue of the spinster state. Queen Elizabeth 1, most famous of all spinsters, was apparently torn between duty and love. In her sensitive and sympathetic biography, published in the 1840s, Mary Agnes Strickland relates the Queen's Address to her House of Commons in response to their petition that she marry and produce royal issue. She told them that:

When she received that ring, she had solemnly bound herself in marriage to the realm; and that it would be quite sufficient for the memorial of her name and for her glory, if, when she died, an inscription were engraved on a marble tomb, saying, 'Here lieth Elizabeth, which reigned a virgin, and died a virgin'.

Elizabeth's conflicts in reaching and living with her decision inspired her to write these and other beautiful love poems:

When I was fair and young and favour graced me
Of many was I sought, their mistress for to be:
But I did scorn them all, and answered them therefore
'Go, go, go, seek some other where:
Importune me no more.'

How many weeping eyes I made to pine with woe
How many sighing hearts, I have no skill to show
Yet I the prouder grew, and answered them therefore,
'Go, go, go, seek some other where:
Importune me no more.'

Then spake fair Venus' son, that proud victorious boy
And said, 'Fine Dame, since that you be so coy,
I will so pluck your plumes that you shall say no more,
'Go, go, go, seek some other where:
Importune me no more.'

When he had spake these words, such change grew in my breast
That neither night nor day, since that, I could take any rest
That lo, I did repent that I had said before,
'Go, go, go, seek some other where:
Importune me no more.'

One man Queen Elizabeth had 'in mind' to marry was Duke Francis of Anjou. He arrived in London to woo her in 1582. But again politics intervened and the Duke demanded leave to depart. Marriage negotiations went on for three years and were very beneficial for British foreign policy. However, when they ceased, and the Duke was no longer a suitor, Elizabeth revealed some of her inner feelings in these verses written on a model of Petrarch.

I grieve, yet dare not shew my discontent;
I love, and yet am forced to seem to hate;
I dote, but dare not what ever I meant;
I seem stark mute, yet inwardly doe prate;
I am, and am not – freeze, and yet I burn;
Since from myself, my other self I turn.

My care is like my shadow in the sun, –
Follows me flying – flies when I pursue it;
Stands and lives by me – does what I have done:
This too familiar care doth make rue it.
No means I find to rid him from my breast,
Till by the end of things it be suppressed.

Some gentler passion steal into my mind,
(For I am soft, and made of melting snow;)
Or be more cruel, love, or be more kind;
Or let me float or sink, be high or low;
Or let me live with some more sweet content;
Or die, and so forget what love e'er meant.

When women seek in each other what they fail to find in relationships with men, do they fare any better? Dorothy L. Sayers, best known for her highly successful detective stories, is sceptical about the possibilities. She writes in a letter to Leonard Green in 1919:

Few friendships between women will stand the strain of being romantically considered – all those I've ever watched have ended in 'dead–sea apples' (sic) and I avoid them like the plague. Men manage better, I think, because most of them spend half their lives in Cloud Cuckoo Land in any case. Of course, there is the amusing Cock and Hen friendship – but it is so like a game of chess.

Katherine Mansfield, on the other hand, describes a quite positive experience of communion between two women in her collection of short stories, Bliss, *published in 1920.*

What she simply couldn't make out – what was miraculous – was how she should have guessed Miss Fulton's mood so exactly and so instantly.

'I believe this does happen very, very rarely between women. Never between men,' thought Bertha. 'But while I am making the coffee in the drawing-room perhaps she will "give a sign".'

What she meant by that she did not know, and what would happen after that she could not imagine.

. . . At that moment Miss Fulton 'gave the sign'. 'Have you a garden?' said the cool sleepy voice.

This was so exquisite on her part that all Bertha could do was to obey. She crossed the room, pulled the curtains apart, and opened those long windows.

'There,' she breathed.

And the two women stood side by side looking at the slender, flowering tree. Although it was so still it seemed like a flame of a candle, to stretch up, to point, to quiver in the bright air, to grow taller and taller as they gazed – almost to touch the rim of the round, silver moon.

How long did they stand there? Both, as it were, caught in that circle of unearthly light, understanding each other perfectly, creatures of another world, and wondering what they were to do in this one with all this blissful treasure that burned in their bosoms and dropped, in silver flowers, from their hair and hands. For ever – for a moment?

Describing her first meeting with Mrs Weston Chapman in Boston in 1834, Harriet Martineau expresses affection for another woman in intimate terms which were rarely, if ever, revealed in her time:

I hear now as I write, the clear silvery tones of her who was to be the friend of the rest of my life. I still see the exquisite beauty which took me by surprise that day: the slender graceful

Plate 6 Two female nudes by Dame Barbara Hepworth, 1949

form – the golden hair which might have covered her to her feet; – the brilliant complexion, noble profile, and deep blue eyes; – the aspect, meant by nature to be soft and winning only, but that day (as ever since) so vivified by courage, and so strengthened by upright conviction, as to appear the very embodiment of heroism.

Harriet Martineau was an energetic journalist and novelist with a passion for social reform that took her into the abolitionist fight in America at considerable personal risk. She, like many of her sex before and after her, sought to push back the barriers that confined woman to the traditional domestic role.

In the seventeeth century Mary Astell made great plans to erect a monastery for those ladies who would desire the advantage of a retreat from the world. The project attracted considerable attention, including that of royalty, but it remained an idealistic dream. Mary Astell is chiefly remembered for her Serious Proposal to the Ladies *in which she wrote:*

No lady of quality should fall in love. Modesty requires that a woman should not fall in love before marriage, but only make choice of one whom she can love hereafter; she who has none but innocent affections being easily able to fix them where Duty requires.

The price of duty is the subject of this monologue from Doris Lessing's play 'Play with a Tiger', published in 1958. Anna speaks aloud her mother's thoughts:

'Yes, that's how I spend my life, pinching and saving – all day cooking and preserving and making clothes for the kids, that's all I ever do, I never even get a holiday. And it's for a man who doesn't even know I'm here - well, if he had to do without me, he'd know what I've done for him. He'd value me if he had to do without me – if I left him he'd know soon enough. There's Mr Jones from the store. He's a soft spot for me, trying to kiss me when there's no one there but us two. Yes I'd just have to lift my finger and Mr Jones would take me away – I didn't lack for men before I married – they came running when I smiled. Ah! God in heaven, if I hadn't married this good-for-nothing here, I'd be a great pianist, I'd know all the golden world – Paris, Rome, London. I'd know the great world, and here I am, stuck in a dump like this with two ungrateful kids and a no-good husband.'

The great actress Mrs Patrick Campbell also felt the frustration of 'a kitchen and four walls'. In a letter to her sister in 1884, shortly after her first child was born, she wrote:

You seem to have so many friends and time to read and paint there I envy you more than I can say – when days and weeks pass in washing and nursing a baby, putting two rooms straight and acting to those around me as though the happiness of my life were complete. I have love, it is true, but love without comfort is a sorry sight – like some beautiful cripple.

Mary Wollstonecraft raised her voice against a system which expected women to love their husbands out of duty. In Mary and the Wrongs of Women, *an autobiographical novel, she outlined her philosophy, drawn directly from her varied experiences of life:*

Those who support a system of what I term false refinement and will not allow a great part of love in the female, as well as male breast, to such observers I have nothing to say, any more than to the moralists, who insist that women ought to, and can love their husbands because it is their duty . . . When novelists or moralists praise as a virtue, a woman's coldness of constitution, and want of passion; and make her yield to the ardour of her lover out of sheer compassion, or to promote a frigid plan of future comfort, I am disgusted. They may be good women, in the ordinary acceptation of the phrase, but they want that fire of the imagination, which produces active sensibility, and positive virtue. How does the woman deserve to be characterized, who marries one man, with a heart and imagination devoted to another? Is she not an object of pity or contempt, when thus sacrilegiously violating the purity of her own feelings? . . . I must insist that a heartless conduct is contrary of virtuous. Truth is the only basis of virtue; and we cannot, without depraving our minds, endeavour to please a lover or husband, but in proportion as he pleases us. Men, more effectually to enslave us, may inculcate this partial morality, and lose sight of virtue in subdividing it into the duties of particular stations; but let us not blush for nature without a cause!

Mary Wollstonecraft, who was a great fighter for the rights of women, was driven to attempted suicide by the neglect of her American lover, Gilbert Imlay, by whom she had a daughter. She died of septicaemia in 1797 at the age of thirty-eight, shortly after her marriage to the philosopher William Godwin and the birth of her second daughter, the future Mary Shelley.

Woman's response to passion and duty is also the subject of Anna Wickham's poem 'The Fired Pot':

In our town people live in rows
The only irregular thing in a street is the steeple
And where that points to, God only knows
And not the poor disciplined people!
And I have watched the women growing old,
Passionate about pins, and pence, and soap,
Till the heart within my wedded breast grew cold,
And I lost hope.
But a young soldier came to our town,
He spoke his mind most candidly.
He asked me quickly to lie down,
And that was very good for me.
For though I gave him no embrace –
Remembering my duty –
He altered the expression of my face
And gave me back my beauty.

Vera Brittain was determined not to let marriage and motherhood crush her independence. In Testament of Youth, *published in 1933, she envisaged the struggle this would produce. Vera Brittain's fiancé was killed in France during World War One. In 1925 she married George Catlin, the political philosopher. Their relationship retained a lasting respect for each other's independence.*

Marriage, for any woman who considered all its implications both for herself and her contemporaries, could never, I now knew, mean a 'living happily ever after'; on the contrary it would involve another protracted struggle, a new fight against the tradition which identified wifehood with the imprisoning limitations of a kitchen and four walls, against the prejudices and regulations which still made success in any field more difficult for the married woman than for the spinster, and penalised motherhood by demanding from it the surrender of disinterested intelligence, the sacrifice of that vitalising experience only to be found in the pursuit of an independent profession. But tired as I was of conflict, I felt that I must not shrink from that fight, the attempt to prove that marriage and motherhood need never tame the mind, nor swamp and undermine ability and training . . . If marriage made the fight harder, so much the better; it would become part of my war and as this I would face it, and show that, however stubborn any domestic problem, a lasting solution could be found if only men and women would seek it together.

Actress Fanny Kemble questioned whether the ideal relationship in which this lasting solution could be found can ever exist or even should exist within the bonds of marriage. This is an excerpt from a letter she wrote in 1837, taken from Fanny Kemble's Records of Later Life *published in 1882.*

A woman should be her husband's best and dearest friend, as he should be hers: but friendship is a relation of equality, in which the same perfect respect for each other's liberty is exercised on both sides; and that sort of marriage, if it exists at all anywhere is, I suspect, very uncommon everywhere. Moreover, I am not sure that marriage ever is, can be, or ought to be such an equality . . . In the relationship of friendship there is perfect freedom, and an undoubted claim on each side to be neither dependent on, nor controlled by, each other's will. In the relation of marriage this is impossible; and therefore certainly marriage is not friendship . . . A woman should, I think, love her husband better than anything on earth except her own soul, which I think a man should respect above everything on earth but his own soul; and there my dear is a very pretty puzzle for you, which a good many people have failed to solve.

Fanny Kemble's own marriage was doomed to failure from the start. In 1833, in America, she married Pierce Butler, a planter from Georgia who turned out to be a slave owner. Fanny had by that time voiced her own abhorrence of slavery and had become famous for her daring outspokenness. She divorced her husband in 1848 and returned to the stage and her writing career to support herself.

This ideal state of equality in love that seemed to elude the poet Christina Rossetti in her own life was celebrated in her sonnet sequence 'Monna Innomonata', from which these lines are taken:

Love me for I love you – and answer
Love me for I love you – so shall we stand
As happy equals in the flowering land
Of Love, that knows no dividing sea.

Happily there are many images of woman satisfied in her married state. Lady Ann Fanshawe seems to have had an ideal relationship with her husband Richard, whom she married in 1644 when she was nineteen and he thirty-five. The marriage lasted twenty-three years and twenty-nine days, when Richard died. Lady Ann wrote this account in her memoirs to her infant son, so that he should know something of his father's character:

Glory be to God we never had but one mind throughout our lives, our souls were wrapped up in each other, our aims and designs were one, our loves one, and our resentments one. We so studied one the other that we knew each other's mind by our looks; whatever was real happiness, God gave it to me in him.

Marie Stopes wanted all women to have greater fulfillment in marriage, and campaigned vigorously for sexual enlightenment and birth control. Her written works have included Married Love, Wise Parenthood *and* Radiant Motherhood. *This excerpt is from* Married Love, *published in 1918:*

The happiness of a perfect marriage, which enhances the vitality of the private life, renders one not only capable of adding to the stream of the life-blood of the community in children, but by marriage one is also rendered a fitter and more perfect instrument for one's own particular work, the results of which should be shared by society as a whole . . .

Elizabeth Barrett Browning described the nurturing quality of mother love in her poem 'Aurora Leigh' published in 1857.

Women know
The way to rear up children (to be just)
They know a simple, merry, tender knack
Of tying sashes, fitting baby shoes,
And stringing pretty words that make no sense,
And kissing full sense into empty words.

For some, motherhood is unwelcome. Lady Ottoline Morrell, famous literary hostess, married to the Liberal MP Phillip Morrell, wrote in her diary in 1905:

I was expecting the arrival of a child and this was not very welcome to me. It seemed an invasion, a burden upsetting the wonderful intimacy and companionship of our life together.

To most mothers I hope it is a lovely and warm invasion, fulfilling their destiny and enlarging their lives. Never did I feel I was bringing a new and beautiful creation into the world. I felt helpless to form or to mould the life that lay dormant within me.

The cruel shock that childbirth can bring to some women is expressed vividly by Mrs Humphry Ward in her novel Robert Elsmere, *which was published in 1888. In this extract, Catherine Elsmere confides to her husband:*

The pain of labour seems to take the joy even out of our love – and the child. I feel ashamed that mere physical pain should have laid such a hold on me – and yet I can't get away from it. It's not for myself. Comparatively I had so little to bear. But I know now for the first time what physical pain may mean and I never knew before. Oh, when I get well, how I will take care of the women here! What women must suffer here, in out-of-the-way cottages – no Doctor, no kind nursing, all that agony and struggle!

Mrs Ward was born into a distinguished intellectual family and married a tutor of an Oxford college. She followed a literary career, producing twenty-eight novels.

A trauma of a different kind faced Mary, Queen of Scots, when she gave birth to her son, Prince James. To dispel malicious gossip she felt obliged to make this public announcement to her husband, Henry Stewart, Earl of Darnley, and surrounding courtiers, at Edinburgh Castle on 19 June 1566:

'My Lord,' she said, 'God has given you and me a son, begotten by none but you. My Lord, I protest to God, and as I shall answer to Him at the Great Day of Judgement, this is your son and no other man's son. And I am desirous that all here, with ladies and others bear witness, for he is so much your son that I fear it will be the worse for him hereafter.'

This is the son who (I hope) shall first unite the two kingdoms of Scotland and England.'

A deeper experience of motherhood emerges from Rosamund Lehmann's short autobiographical work The Swan in the Evening, *published in 1967.*

When I came round from the anaesthetic that late afternoon in January 1934, there was no nurse or doctor in the room. She and I were alone. I heard her before I saw her. She was making strong, broken noises of protest, sorrow, from some unidentifiable region near my bed.

'Yes, yes I know,' I said. 'Never mind, I know.'

Immediately she was silent, listening. In this soundless naught recognition started to vibrate like a fine filament between us; quickened, tautened. I swung in living darkness, emptiness, in the beginning of the deepest listening of my life.

When, probably quite soon, Sister came in and said loudly, 'Here's your baby, dear – a lovely daughter. Don't you want to see her?' I started to sob. I suppose for happiness.

In times of despair and depression woman can question the very act of procreation. Sheila Macleod, writing in our own times, captures the depths of these feelings in her Letters from the Portuguese, *published in 1971. Emily Bastion plans her own death and writes to her husband:*

Oh Robert, what a terrible crime we commit every time we bring a child into this world. We do it so unthinkingly, so unheedingly. And what's more, we actually rejoice at the advent of yet another human being. We congratulate ourselves on our achievement. The baby itself has no choice in the matter. It must live if it is healthy. It must make the same hazardous and crippling journey that we made through childhood and adolescence into doubtful maturity. That is where I am at now. My eyes are opened. And I can see that the world is full of injustice and cruelty and pain. That is the general rule. Anything else is just a temporary respite. Knowing all this how can I believe that it will be any different for the beings I myself have given birth to? We should ask our children for forgiveness instead of gratitude.

Certainly many women, like Queen Victoria, find their children a burden. She wrote this poignant admission in a letter to her daughter, the Crown Princess of Prussia, in 1868:

I assure you children are more anxiety and sorrow than pleasure. When they grow up, their divided interests prevent them even understanding what a parent suffers and feels. When one's Beloved husband is gone and one's children are married one feels that a friend, near your own age, and one who can devote him or herself entirely to you, is the one thing you do require to help you on – and sympathise entirely with you. Not that you love your children less, but you feel that, as they grow up and marry, you can be of so little use to them, and they to you, and that they do what they like, and how many break their parents' hearts. You will say I paint a dreary picture but I fear it is not untrue. As long as children are young all that is different.

And yet the will to have a child and to nurture it can be phenomenally strong. Mrs Gaskell typifies this in one of the characters in her novel Cranford, *published as a series of contributions to the magazine* Household Words *starting in 1851. This is a part of Mrs Brown's story in that book:*

Yes! Six children died off, like little buds nipped untimely, in that cruel India . . . And when Phoebe was coming, I said to my husband, 'Sam, when the child is born, and I am strong, I

Plate 7 ‘Before going to Bed’ by Queen Victoria, 1843

shall leave you; it will cut my heart cruel; but if this baby dies too, I shall go mad . . . I will save, and I will hoard, and I will beg – and I will die, to get a passage home to England, where our baby may live.' God bless him! he said I might go . . . I set off . . . from station to station, from Indian village to village, I went along carrying my child . . . And the natives were very kind. We could not understand one another; but they saw my baby on my breast, and they came out to me and brought me rice and milk and sometimes flowers . . . and they wanted me to stay with them . . . but it seemed to me as if Death was following me to take my baby away from me . . . and I thought how God had cared for mothers ever since the world was made, and would care for me . . . When I knew I had only two days' journey more before me, I could not help it, ma'am – it might be idolatry, I cannot tell – but I was near one of the native temples, and I went in it with my baby to thank God for his great mercy; for it seemed to me that where others had prayed before to their God, in their joy or in their agony, was of itself a sacred place . . . And in two years' time Sam earned his discharge, and came home to me, and to our child.

Mrs Gaskell was a great humanitarian whose literary works promoted social harmony. Her husband was a minister. They had four daughters, and a son who died in infancy.

Little is known about the life of Julian of Norwich, one of the greatest British mystics six hundred years ago, except that she lived most of her life as a recluse. She recorded a series of spiritual revelations she experienced in Revelations of Divine Love, *a masterpiece of literature, in which she describes visions she received during a severe illness. These visions lasted several hours and were of Christ's Passion, The Holy Trinity and the Virgin Mother. Julian of Norwich uses the image of the instinctive love between mother and child to equate the love of Jesus for mankind with the nurturing love of the Virgin Mother:*

Fair and sweet is our heavenly Mother in the sight of our soul; precious and lovely are the gracious children in the sight of our heavenly Mother, with mildness and meekness and all the fair virtues that belong in kind, to children. For kindly the children despair not of the mother's love, kindly the child presumeth not of itself, kindly the child loveth the mother and each one of them the other. These are the fair virtues (with all others that are like to them) wherewith our heavenly Mother is served and pleased. And I understood that there is no higher stature in this life than childhood – in the feebleness and failing of might and understanding – until the time that our gracious Mother hath brought us up to our Father's bliss. And there shall truly be made known to us his meaning, in the sweet words where he saith: 'All shall be well; and thou shalt see it thyself that all manner of thing shall be well.'

3
Aspirations and achievements

It emerges that woman has long recognised in herself a potential outside her traditional family role. Historical records from Anglo-Saxon times to the present day give accounts of women looking to fulfil possibilities they see in themselves as ruler and diplomat, artist and artisan, academic and adventurer. In all, woman is seeking to fulfil self and to be mistress of her own destiny.

Attitudes and customs of society, male supremacy and even conflicts in her own nature prove formidable obstacles for woman as she seeks to go beyond the traditional mould. Not least of these has been the degradation and exploitation of women which at times in our history has reached alarming proportions. Only a hundred years ago or less, education was still a privilege for the rich or kept for sons and brothers; women had no voice in politics and were prevented from entering any professional career. At times women have been little more than cheap labour for the growing industrial centres, or chattels of husbands who believed in their own unquestionable superiority. The Law was heavily biased in favour of men until recent times; most women were afraid to speak out, however much they and their children suffered from cruelty or deprivation.

Many women responded with a single-minded purpose to the challenge of such conditions, as many today seek to end the remaining injustices and inequalities between the sexes. Their response gives us not only great personal achievements to admire and emulate, but also major advances along the road to greater social, personal, economic and political freedom for women. How remarkable it is that just over sixty-seven years

Plate 8 'A Lady Reading' by Gwen John, 1907–8

ago women were fighting for the right to vote in this country's elections, and today we have a woman Prime Minister.

A great many of the challenges facing women today arise directly from the rights and freedoms which have been dearly won by the women of yesterday, as they responded to their realisation that there is more to woman than domesticity. Virginia Woolf describes graphically in her Professions for Women, *published in 1931, the conditions that so many find unacceptable.*

The phantom was woman, and when I came to know her better I called her after the heroine of a famous poem, 'The Angel in the House'. It was she who used to come between me and my paper when I was writing reviews. It was she who bothered me and wasted my time and so tormented me that at last I killed her . . . I will describe her as shortly as I can. She was immensely charming. She was utterly unselfish. She excelled in the difficult arts of family life. She sacrificed herself daily. If there was a chicken, she took the leg. If there was a draught, she sat in it – in short she was so constituted that she never had a mind or a wish of her own . . . Above all – I need not say it – she was pure. In those days, the last of Queen Victoria – every house had its Angel.

So much of that 'phantom' is a part of every woman's nature and many have not found it easy, or even desirable, to kill her off.

Charlotte Brontë's heroine Shirley, in her novel of that name, is mirroring Charlotte's own longings for a life beyond the restrictions of the conventions of her time. Shirley *was published in 1849.*

'It makes me long to travel, Miss Helstone.'

'When you are a woman, perhaps you may be able to gratify your wish.'

'I mean to make a way to do so, if one is not made for me. I cannot always live in Briarfield. The whole world is not very large compared with creation. I must see the outside of our own round planet at least.'

'How much of its outside?'

'First, this hemisphere where we live, then the other. I am resolved that my life shall be a life; not a black trance like the toad's buried in marble, nor a long slow death like yours in Briarfield Rectory.'

'Like mine. What can you mean, child?'

'Might you not as well be tediously dying as for ever shut up in that glebe house, a place that, when I pass, always reminds me of a windowed grave? I never see any movement about the door. I never hear a sound from the wall; I believe smoke never issues from the chimneys. What do you do there?'

'I sew, I read, I learn lessons.'

'Are you happy?'

'Should I be happier wandering alone in strange countries as you wish to do?'

'Much happier, even if you did nothing but wander . . . if you only went on and on like some enchanted lady in a fairy tale, you might be happier than now . . . you would pass many a hill, wood, water course, each perpetually altering in aspect. Nothing changes at Briarfield Rectory.'

'Is change necessary to happiness?'

'Yes.'

'Is it synonymous with it?'

'I don't know – but I feel monotony and death to be almost the same.'

Early in the eighteenth century this chafing against the accepted 'lot' of women was expressed by Ann Finch, Countess of Winchelsea, renowned poetess. She holds up the example of Deborah, the Israelite prophetess and stateswoman of the twelfth century BC, *for women to emulate in her poem:*

> Goodbreeding, fassion, dancing, dressing, play
> Are the accomplishements we shou'd desire;
> To write, or read, or think, or to enquire
> wou'd cloud our beauty, and exaust our time,
> And interrupt the Conquests of our prime;
> Whilst the dull manage of a servile house
> Is held by some, our outmost art, and use,
> Sure 'twas not ever thus, nor are we told
> Fables, of Women that excell'd of old;
> To whom, by the diffusive hand of Heaven
> Some share of witt, and poetry was given . . .

A Woman here, leads fainting Israel on,
She fights, she wins, she tryumphs with a song,
Devout, Majestick, for the subject fitt,
And far about her arms, exalts her witt,
Then, to the peacefull, shady Palm withdraws,
And rules the rescu'd Nation, with her Laws,
How are we fal'n! by fal'n mistaken rules,
And Education's, more than Nature's fools,
Debarr'd from all improve-ments of the mind
And to be dull, expected and dessigned;
And if some one would soar above the rest,
With warmer fancy, and ambition pressed,
So strong the opposing faction still appears,
The hopes to thrive can ne'er outweigh the fears.

Elizabeth Fry's efforts to improve the state of prisons and conditions of deported convicts, led her to be specific in suggesting roles for women in society outside the home. In her Observations on the Visiting, Superintendence and Government of Female Prisoners, *published in 1827, she writes:*

I wish to make a few remarks . . . respecting my own sex, and the place which I believe it to be their duty and privilege to fill in the scale of society. Far be it from me to tempt them to forsake their right province. My only desire is that they should fill that province well; and although their calling in many respects, materially differs from that of the other sex and is not so exalted a one yet . . . if adequately fulfilled, it has nearly, if not quite, an equal influence on society . . .

No person will deny the importance attached to the character and conduct of a woman in all her domestic and social relations, when she is filling the station of a daughter, a sister, a wife, a mother or a mistress of a family. But it is a dangerous error to suppose that the duties of females end here . . . no persons appear to me to possess so strong a claim on their compassion . . . as the helpless, the ignorant, the afflicted or the depraved of their own sex . . . During the last ten years much attention has been successfully bestowed by women on the female inmates of our prisons . . . But a similar care is evidently needed for our hospitals, our lunatic asylums and our workhouses . . . Were ladies to make a practice of regularly visiting them, a most important check would be obtained on a variety of abuses, which are far too apt to creep into the management of these establishments . . .

Elizabeth Fry was a Quaker reformer and successful preacher who, as well as her prison work, helped vagrants in London and Brighton. Unlike Virginia Woolf, she is careful to advocate that women still continue to fulfil the domestic role as conscientiously as ever, and to take up their social responsibilities as an 'extra'.

Vera Brittain brings together some of the problems and solutions facing women in their search for independence and fulfilment in a man's world. This extract is taken from Lady into Woman, *published in 1953.*

How can woman achieve greatness in an art or profession without sacrificing human relationships in the process? This problem is even more fundamental than the struggle for equal pay . . . In theory the justice of equal opportunity is accepted, in practice the opportunities themselves are curtailed by traditional assumptions. These do not survive in men alone; the most gifted women still suffer from perennial conflict with an inculcated ideal of feminine duty which demands not achievement but self sacrifice . . . Must we then accept the proposition that a woman writer can produce great literature only by subduing her natural desire for children? To do so would be defeatism . . . Such sacrifice is itself a challenge which demands the pursuit of new solutions . . . Above all else is needed the creation, through education and training, of a co-operative home atmosphere . . . So long as women writers and artists must sacrifice motherhood in order to fulfil the inexorable demands of a creative gift the feminist revolution remains incomplete. With the answer to this problem the future of Woman now rests.

Doris Lessing points us to the 'great line of women' who have realised their potential and who can point the way for us to follow. This excerpt comes from A Golden Notebook, *probably Doris Lessing's best-known work, published in 1962:*

In what way are you different? Are you saying there haven't

been artist-women before? There haven't been women who were independent? There haven't been women who insisted on sexual freedom? I tell you, there are a great line of women stretching out behind you into the past, and you have to seek them out and find them in yourself and be conscious of them.

This great line of women can be seen as part of an ongoing movement stretching across centuries – what novelist and journalist Geraldine Jewsbury calls a development of womanhood itself. This paragraph is taken from a letter she wrote to her close friend Jane Carlyle, wife of the philosopher Thomas Carlyle, in 1850:

We are indications of a development of womanhood which is not yet recognised. It has, so far, no ready channels to run in. But still we have looked and tried and found that the present rules for women will not hold us – that something better and stronger is needed . . . There are women to come after us, who will approach nearer the fullness of the measure of the stature of a woman's nature. I regard myself as a mere indication, a rudiment of the idea, of certain higher qualities and possibilities that are in women.

The achievements of each woman in this development can only be measured against the general conditions they find themselves in or, as Virginia Woolf puts it in one of her Collected Essays *published in 1931:*

The extraordinary woman depends on the ordinary woman. It is only when we know what were the conditions of the average woman's life – the number of her children, whether she had money of her own, if she had a room to herself, whether she had help in bringing up of her family, (if she had servants, whether part of the housework was her task) – it is only then, when we can measure the way of life and the experience of life made possible to the ordinary woman that we can account for the success or failure of the extraordinary woman.

The motivating power of woman's self-awareness and self-belief, prelude to great achievement, is captured by Katherine Mansfield in The Flowering of the Self, *written in 1920:*

True to oneself – Which self? – Which of the many? For what with repressions and reactions and vibrations and reflections there are moments when I feel I am nothing but the small clerk of some hotel without a proprietor who has all his work cut out to enter names and hand the keys to wilful guests . . . Our persistent yet mysterious belief in Self which is continuous and permanent pushes a green spear through the dead leaves and mud, through the years of darkness. And then one day, the light discovers it and shakes the flower free and we are alive, we are flowering for our moment upon the earth. This is the moment after all we live for.

It is in their 'flowering' for their 'moment upon the earth' that we find outstanding women, each giving a unique image of accomplishment and success.

Queen Elizabeth 1, architect of our country's Renaissance, excelled as stateswoman, politician, poetess, musician, patroness. Her quality of resolve shows through in this part of her famous speech as she rallied her troops at Tilbury before they joined battle with the Armada in 1588:

'Let tyrants fear. I have always so behaved myself that, under God I have placed my chiefest strength and safeguard in the loyal hearts and good-will of my subjects, and therefore I have come amongst you, as you see, at this time, not for my recreation and disporting, but being resolved in the midst and heat of the battle to live or die amongst you all, to lay down for my God, and for my Kingdom and for my people, my honour and my blood even in the dust. I know I have the body of a weak and feeble woman, but I have the heart and stomach of a King and a King of England too, and I think foul scorn that Parma, or Spain or any prince of Europe dare to invade the borders of my realm.'

Florence Nightingale employed her talents within the narrow scope open to girls in the nineteenth century and learned how to improve the care for the sick in hospitals. With ten years experience behind her, in 1854 she answered government pleas for help by collecting around her a team of women who could face the horrors of nursing the wounded in the primitive and dangerous conditions of the Crimean War. An assistant nurse to Florence describes how 'The Lady of the Lamp' went about her task:

There was never a severe case of any kind that escaped her notice. It seemed an endless walk and one not easily forgotten. As we slowly passed along, the silence was profound. Very seldom did a moan or cry from those deeply suffering fall on our ears. A dim light burned here and there. Miss Nightingale carried her lantern which she would set down before she bent over any of the patients. I much admired her manner to the men. It was so tender and kind.

Emmeline Pankhurst took the emancipation of women as her objective in life. As leader of the militant suffragette movement which began among Lancashire working women, she adopted sensational methods of propaganda, created traumatic 'happenings', interrupted meetings and often ended up in prison. She toured the United States to arouse interest in the movement and to raise funds. Her efforts were constantly inspired by the plight of women: just how deeply this affected her is described by her daughter, Sylvia, in 1905.

Far into the night my mother railed against the treachery of men and bemoaned the impotence of women: 'Poor Women'. The overburdened mothers, the sweated workers, the outcasts of the streets, the orphan children of the workhouse, all mingled in the imagery of her discourse. She appeared so greatly to distress herself that I feared for her health and her reason. On some later occasion, when after a night of these agonies . . . she began again to declaim, I gazed at her in sorrowful concern . . . Suddenly turning on me with a smile, she struck me lightly on the arm. 'Don't look at me like that! Bless you, your old mother likes it. This is what I call Life!'

Evangeline Booth was dedicated to a different cause. She became the first woman General of the Salvation Army in 1934. This excerpt is from the Covenant she made before a meeting of the Army Commissionaires when she assumed office.

'I will seek to preach among you the truth as it is in Christ Jesus. Every impulse of my being shall be to this end. Every talent I possess, every physical, mental and spiritual gift with which God has endowed me, I consecrate to this one purpose.'

'I will ask no privileges, I will seek no honours, I will accept no benefits, I will look for no friend . . . You will ever find me in the front. You will find me in the foremost line of our warfare's most heated conflict, whatever form that conflict may take. This General-arrangement is the nearest to the marriage-altar I have ever come. You have to take me for "better or for worse". Now try me and see how much "better" you will find me, and how little "worse". If more worse than you expect, it won't last long. But do not let anyone set his heart against me before I get started.'

Gertrude Bell achieved the distinction of taking as brilliant a First in Modern History as has ever been taken by any woman at Oxford. This she accomplished before the age of twenty. Gertrude Bell spent a great deal of her life suffering hardship and even imprisonment to satisfy her ambition to travel in Central Arabia. Her life was influenced by her love for a married man, for whom she wrote her diary. This extract she wrote from Amman on 11 January 1914:

Once in the desert I shall be surprised if I do not go where I please. Yes, I know what you thought when you looked at the Taj at dawn, and I love you for wishing I had been with you. There are few people whom one wants at those moments. I have known loneliness in solitude now, for the first time, and in the long days of camel riding, and the long evenings of winter camping, my thoughts have gone wandering far from the campfire into places which I wish were not so full of acute sensation. Sometimes I have gone to bed with a heart so heavy that I thought I could not carry it through the next day. Then comes the dawn, soft and beneficent, stealing over the wide plain and down the long low slopes of the little hollows; and in the end it steals into my dark heart also. I am not a philosopher, but I remember at those times, and am glad to remember, that we count for little. The earth goes on, clothes herself at every dawn with fresh beauty, and rejoices to herself. Our dark hearts cast no shadow over her, and our heavy steps are not felt. And I walk on through the sunlight, comforted – that's the best I can make of it, taught at least some wisdom by solitude, taught submission, and how to bear pain without crying out.

Gertrude Bell promoted the cause of political independence for the Arab peoples and was founder of the National Museum in Baghdad. Her presence and dynamism are captured in Vita Sackville West's description from A Passenger to Teheran, *written in 1925:*

I had known her first in Constantinople, where she arrived straight out of the desert, with all the evening dresses and cutlery and napery that she insisted on taking with her on her wanderings: and then in England, but here she was in her right place, in Iraq, in her own house, with her office in the City, and her white pony in a corner of the garden, and her Arab servants, and her English books, and her Babylonian shards on the mantle piece, and her long thin nose, and her irrepressible vitality. I felt all my loneliness and despair lifted from me in a second. Had it been very hot in the Gulf? got fever had I? but quinine would put that right; and a sprained ankle – too bad! and would I like breakfast first, or a bath? and I would like to see the museum wouldn't I? did I know she was Director of Antiquities in Iran? wasn't that a joke? and would I like to come to tea with the King?

Vita Sackville West also travelled widely as the wife of Harold Nicolson, a British diplomat. She published her experiences as well as writing novels and poetry.

Mary Kingsley was another intrepid traveller. After a sheltered childhood in the academic environment of Cambridge, she set out alone for West Africa in 1893. She financed her trip by undertaking to gather data for Cambridge University. She recorded this account in her journal of her explorations, and her experiences among the tribe known as the Fans:

The next morning the Fans turned their attention on me and started selling to me their store of Elephant tusks and India rubber. I did not want those things then, but felt too nervous to point this out firmly and so had to buy . . . I gradually found myself the proud owner of balls of rubber and a tooth or so, and alas! my little stock of trading cloth and tobacco all going fast. Now to be short of money anywhere is bad, but to be short of money in a Fan village is extremely bad because these Fans when a trader has no more goods to sell them, are liable to start trade all over again by killing him and taking back their ivory and rubber and keep it till another trader comes along . . . All my trade stuff was now exhausted, and I had to start selling my own belongings, and for the first time in my life felt the want of a big outfit. A dozen white ladies blouses sold well, I cannot say they looked well when worn by a brawny warrior in conjunction with nothing else but red paint and a bunch of leopard tails. But I did not hint at this, and I quite realise that a pair of stockings can be made to go further by using them one at a time and putting the top part over the head and letting the rest of the garment float in the breeze . . . The last thing I parted with was my tooth brush, and the afternoon that it had gone, down came the canoe, just as I was making up my mind to set up business as a witch-doctor.

On her return to England, this remarkable woman lectured on her experiences. In 1899 she returned to South Africa, where she died from overwork nursing Boer War prisoners.

In every branch of the arts there have been women who have recognised and realised their creative potential, often against formidable odds. The result is our heritage of masterpieces of literature, poetry, music, painting, sculpture, theatre and ballet.

Dame Margot Fonteyn's autobiography records the life of one of our most talented and celebrated artists. This account describes her performance at the Metropolitan Opera House in 1949:

It was a sweltering hot October night, an Indian summer. The atmosphere inside the Opera House was like a jungle minutes before a tropical storm. When I ran out on to the stage there was a burst of sound. It drowned out the music and also some part of my mind, for I have never been able to remember anything between those first minutes of deafening applause on my entrance, and the incredible reception after the third-act *pas de deux*. It must have been the sheer unexpectedness of it that induced that trance-like state. Unimaginable success! It was unlike anything I had ever experienced before.

The storm had broken. There were flowers everywhere.

Everyone was hysterical. Crowds tried to reach the dressing rooms; the doormen panicked and held distinguished visitors at bay in the street. I felt like a person reprieved from the gallows. With the weight of fear removed, I could have risen straight up through the ceiling. An over-riding thirst made me almost inarticulate. 'Thank you, thank you, thank you' was all I could mumble as a stream of people proffered their congratulations.

Kathleen Ferrier reached similar heights in musical performance. Her memory is kept alive for us in recordings. In a BBC programme broadcast in 1948, she recalled how she felt when first asked to sing in opera:

'I was asked if I would consider singing the part of Lucretia [in Benjamin Britten's "The Rape of Lucretia"]. Heavens, what thoughts raced through my mind. Could I ever walk on a stage without falling over my own rather large feet, not to mention having to sing at the same time . . . It was to be at Glyndebourne . . . After we had settled down and unpacked, notices were posted on various doors about rehearsals. My first day I couldn't believe how difficult it was just to do the simplest arm movements without feeling like a broken down windmill.

'The dress rehearsal came . . . I missed an entry. Then having stabbed myself I fell like a hard dinner roll. After this I thought it time I shuffled off this mortal coil and did an Ophelia-like exit into the lake with only a belligerent swan for company. Whattalife! Oh for a peaceful "Messiah".'

This is one of the humorous anecdotes and accounts of rich musical experience published in Winifred Ferrier's The Life of Kathleen Ferrier. *Illness and an untimely death in 1953 brought an end to a life that has given us some of the best musical performances of this century.*

Ethel Smyth was composing music in the 1930s. She said:

'So far, admission to the house of music on equal terms with men is unthinkable for a composer of my sex.'

In pursuit of self-awareness, Ethel Smyth recommends women look into their own creative origins, asking them to struggle to

Plate 9 'In England's Green and Pleasant Land' by Gluck, 1944

possess their past, their 'mothers', in order to forge the future. In Female Pipings in Eden *she writes:*

Let her once more take up her hollow reed and start afresh. And if Adam should again awake and bid her stop that horrible noise Eve need not be rude. Let her merely say *dolce senza espressione*, 'My dear Adam, if you don't admire my tunes I don't always admire yours. But don't threaten, as you once did, to make this particular horrible noise yourself, for it's my own composition and I hold the copyright. Besides which you couldn't make it yourself if you tried. Some other tune, yes. But not this . . .'

Dame Barbara Hepworth recognised it was her self-discipline that enabled her to become a major twentieth-century sculptress and yet still enjoy many years of happy family life.

It made a firm foundation for my working life – and it formed my idea that a woman artist is not deprived by cooking and having children, nor by nursing children with measles (even in triplicate), one is in fact nourished by this rich life, provided one always does some work each day, even a single half hour, so that the images grow in one's mind. I detest a day of no work, no music, no poetry.

Friends and relations always said to me that it was impossible to be dedicated to any art and enjoy marriage and children. This is untrue, as I had nearly thirty years of wonderful family life; but I will confess that the dictates of work are as compelling for a woman as for a man. Not competitively, but as complementary, and this is only just being realised.

These extracts are taken from Dame Barbara's A Pictorial Autobiography, *published in 1970. She spent the main part of her working life in St Ives in Cornwall.*

The compelling need to work, which Dame Barbara identifies, has taken women into competition with men, often on unequal and discriminatory terms. It was inevitable that 'equality' should become a major goal in woman's struggle to use her talents and skills, even from the earliest days. So accepted was the 'maleness' of the creative need that Aphra Behn, writing in

1686, referred to it as 'the masculine part' of her. In the preface to her play 'Lucky Chance' she writes:

All I ask, is the privilege for the masculine part, the poet in me . . . If I must not, because of my sex, have this freedom, I lay down my quill and you shall hear no more of me, no, not so much as to make comparisons, because I will be kinder to my brothers of the pen, than they have been to a defenseless woman, for I am not content to write for a third day only. I value fame as much as if I had been born a hero; and if you rob me of that, I can retire from the ungrateful world and scorn its fickle favours.

Aphra Behn met with much hostility and derision in her writing career, a career in which she achieved success as novelist, playwright and poet. She led a life of high adventure, and was employed by Charles II as a spy in Antwerp during the outbreak of the Dutch-English wars.

Many women have succeeded in their careers with the love and support of their families. Julia Cameron was forty-eight years old in 1863 when her daughter gave her a camera saying 'It may amuse you, Mother, to try to photograph during your solitude at Freshwater.' In her Selected Writings *Julia Cameron recounts this incident and how it led her to become a portrait photographer of considerable fame.*

The gift from those I loved so tenderly added more and more impulse to my deeply seated love of the beautiful, and from the first moment I handled my lens with a tender ardour, and it has become to me as a living thing, with voice and memory and vigour.

I longed to arrest all beauty that came before me, and at length the longing has been satisfied.

My first picture was a portrait of a farmer of Freshwater, who, to my fancy, resembled Bolingbroke. The peasantry of our island is very handsome . . . This farmer I paid half-a-crown an hour, and, after many half crowns and many hours spent in experiments, I got my first picture, and this was the one I effaced when holding it triumphantly to dry.

I turned my coal-house into my dark-room, and a glazed fowl-house I had given to my children became my glass house!

Having succeeded with one farmer, I next tried two children . . . I took one child alone, appealing to her feelings and telling her of the waste of poor Mrs Cameron's chemicals and strength if she moved. The appeal had its effect, and I now produced a picture which I called 'My First Success'. I was in a transport of delight . . . Sweet, sunny haired little Annie! No later prize has effaced the memory of this joy.

Many women have accepted a secondary position to men in their professional working life. Caroline Herschel was one. Like her brother William, she started life as a musician in Hanover, Germany. When William settled in England and started his work on astronomy he made it possible for Caroline to join him and to share in this great enterprise. Caroline Herschel once observed: 'All I am, all I know, I owe to my brother.'

She was always in a subservient position to her brother but nevertheless Caroline Herschel was the first woman to discover comets, eight in all, and fourteen nebulae. King George IV honoured her work and presented her with a small stipend. The Royal Astronomical Society made her an honorary member at a time when women were not allowed full membership. In her own words, her epitaph says:

The eyes of her who is glorified here below turned to the starry heavens. Her own discoveries of comets and her participation in the immortal labours of her brother bear witness of this to future eyes.

In the seventeenth century Margaret, Duchess of Newcastle, refers to discrimination against her sex at that time in her autobiographical Memoirs.

It will satisfy me if my writings please the readers, though not the learned; for I had rather be praised in this by the most, although not the best; for all I desire is fame, and fame is nothing but a great noise, and noise lives most in a multitude. I confess that my ambition is restless and not ordinary, because, it would have an extraordinary fame; and since all heroic actions, public employment, powerful governments and eloquent pleadings are denied our sex in this age, this is the cause I write so much.

Geraldine Jewsbury knew the hazards facing women with ambition. She wrote about them in a letter to her close friend Jane Welsh Carlyle on 6 September 1850:

When women get to be energetic, strong characters with reputations of their own, and live in the world with business to attend to, they all do get in the habit of making use of people and of taking care of themselves in a way that is startling! And yet how are they to help it? If they are thrown into the world, they must swim for their life. In short whenever a woman gets to be a personage in any shape it makes her hard and unwomanly in some point or other.

Even in politics, women have proved that they can get to the top. It is an achievement that in 1943 Margot Asquith could not envisage:

No amount of education will make women first-rate politicians. Can you see a woman becoming a Prime Minister? I cannot imagine a greater calamity for these islands were they to be put under the guidance of a woman at 10 Downing Street. They are not even good speakers.

Margot Asquith, Countess of Oxford, was the second wife of Herbert Henry Asquith, Prime Minister of Britain from 1908 to 1916. Her comments are made in her memoirs Off the Record, *published in 1943. It has taken less than forty years to nullify that opinion. Putting aside party political prejudice, we recognise Margaret Thatcher as one of the most outstanding national and international leaders of this century. She gave the following comments on her life and work in an interview for Central Television in 1986.*

'You do not think in terms of being a woman Prime Minister or a woman Minister or a woman Member of Parliament. You think in terms of "This is my job, how am I going to achieve my objectives? How best can I do it? What is the best way to do it?".'

'Oh yes, you know, you will quite often hear people say: "Well look, she is the best man in politics" and I say: "Oh no, much better than that; she is the best woman". It is extraordinary you still hear that, but look, I never know, I never quite understand why. Running a family – supposing you have a large family, women have to be very firm; they could not do it otherwise. They have to be very decisive; they could not do it otherwise. Those are natural qualities in women, natural, and a woman who helps with the family business has to be very firm. A woman who becomes a widow has to be extremely firm, but no one suggests she is masculine. No one suggests that because she has to make tough, difficult decisions that she is not kind. I think it is because we have not yet got enough women getting to the top and therefore people tend to think it is unusual. It is not unusual, and many of the qualities which we display quite naturally in our jobs here are just those very same qualities that a woman who is running a home, who is after all a good manager – that is what running a home well means – a good manager, has to display in the home.

Sheila Scott, OBE, became a skilled pilot. She has given us an account of her long-distance flights between London and Australia in the 1960s, and her solo flight in a light aircraft over the North Pole. She has described her exciting adventures and also her growing understanding of herself as she dared these feats of endurance. This passage is taken from On Top of the World, *published in 1973:*

I have known in a small way what it is to be alone – seemingly completely alone in the accepted sense – in my aircraft hundreds of miles from sight of human eyes, or sound of human voice. I had to discover for myself what this was like, but in fact by doing this very thing I learnt it was but an infinitesimal part of understanding.

Previously I had been fighting mythical giants and devils, but I had always used the same vehicle – my aircraft. But even the aircraft itself is subject to many influences which in turn influence me, and so however dedicated, and even by using the same vehicle to learn more about your personal aims, you can be greatly misled.

I am just beginning to understand that there can be many other areas and vehicles in oneself. One can always go on discovering more and it possibly required far more discipline and courage to do it in this more simple way. Discipline to prevent your imagination going wild and to stick to the aims you have set yourself; courage is required in all kinds of ways, sometimes even in homely ways such as when and whether you should be leaving your room or deserting your studies to please others . . . Just like the pilot, somehow, I struggle through, and find a landfall, though not necessarily the piece of land that I was aiming for, nevertheless smooth enough to get down on and often find an unexpected experience – and so I refuel and take off once again to continue with my quest.

Joanna Field, too, found a simple way to discover what were the controlling factors in her life. She made lists: lists of things she liked, hated, planned, wanted or feared. They were published in A Life of One's Own *in 1934, and can be instantly identified with*:

Things I Love

Flowers, light and colours.
The patience of cart-horses.
The abandon and moods of dogs.
Sharing an idea in conversation when minds move together.
Bodily sensations, hot sun, wind, rhythm, relaxation after exercise, water and fire.
The sense of strangers' moods arising from a glimpse of their faces and attitudes.
Confidences from people – strangers or friends.
Companionably sharing things, forestalling someone's need.
Getting at what someone is driving at in a play or picture.
Fairs, loitering in a crowd.
Beginning nice things.
Old implements.
Traditional knowledge for tilling the soil, seamanship and crafts: as opposed to efficiency methods.
Intricate mechanisms that are not man made.
Freedom from possessions.
Buying things.
Good food.
Laughing.

Hands on human skin.
Attraction towards a person.
A new idea when first it is grasped.
People singing out of doors.
Clean clothes.

Things I hate

Things that are meaningless and full of detail.
Suburban roads and houses.
Lace curtains.
Being bored.
Fussy dresses.
Making a fool of myself.
Being laughed at.
Being disapproved of.
Glaring lights, unshaded.
Being copied in my attempts to be original.
Being made to feel conspicuous.
Old society ladies.
Frittering time on household necessities especially when it's fine.
Spending a lot of money on something I don't like.
Being cold, having wet feet.
Being conspicuous, having arguments in public places or being unsuitably dressed.
Having my taste or actions criticised.
Quarrels between my friends.
People taking it for granted that they can share my things.
Being made use of.
Earnest, dowdy or arty women.
Pompous men.
Velvet and plush chairs.
The suggestion or feeling that you are dominated by anyone.
Hearing about the good times anyone is having if you consider those people your equals or inferiors in general.

Plans

– to have enough money to have a child
– to dress moderately well
– to know what is going on in the world
– to be able to talk well
– to get to know M. better
– to answer my letters

– to feel at ease and adequate with all people I meet
– to do things because I really want to and not because other people do them or to please them
– to read French easily
– to express my feelings, be impulsive and emotional not consistent and aloof
– to be able to detect and bring out the significant things in people I meet; not miss 'so much and so much' through blindness and egocentricity

. . . I had never been able to decide which one of these could be made the central purpose of my life . . . at that time I could not understand at all that my real purpose might be to learn to have no purposes . . . I began to have an idea of my life not as the slow shaping of achievement to fit my preconceived purposes, but as the gradual discovery and growth of a purpose which I did not know. It will mean walking in a fog for a bit but it's the only way which is not a presumption – forcing the self into a theory . . .

Fears and drawing-back

Of being tied up, of limiting my will, no longer a 'mobile unit' to come and go as I choose.
Of limitations in future friendships.
Of being spoken to in the streets – I want to hide.
That people we have social introductions to will think we do not know how to behave.
That I'll go into a restaurant not meant for women or something like that and get stared at.
That I'll be conspicuous.
I dithered on the pavement before crossing the street.
I was afraid of asking for information.
I was afraid to go along the day coach to the women's toilet past rows of people.

Wants

– a lover
– a perfect companion
– to be famous for some service to the race, a great pioneer work
– a great many friends
– to achieve a unique work of art
– to 'plumb to the depths of human experience'

– to be recognised as a unique individual
– to be in people's confidence.

. . . It was far easier to want what other people seemed to want and then imagine that the choice was one's own. I want time, leisure to draw and study a few things closely, by feeling, not thinking, to get at things. I want laughter, its satisfaction and balance and a wide security. I want a chance to play, to do things I choose just for the joy of doing, for no other purpose or advancement.

To understand patiently the laws of growing things.
To live in a regular rhythm with sun and rain and wind and fresh air and the coming and going of the seasons. I want few friends that I may learn to know and understand and talk to without embarrassment or doubt.
I want to write books, to see them printed and bound. And to get clearer ideas on this great tangle of human behaviour.
To simplify my environment so that a vacillating will is kept in the ways I love.

Joanna Field came to discover that 'the growth of understanding follows an ascending spiral rather than a straight line'!

Jane Austen's letters to her friends and to her sister Cassandra reveal her thoughts and describe her pastimes. In 1801 she wrote: 'I have now attained the art of letter writing, which we are always told is to express on paper exactly what one would say to the same person by word of mouth.' Literary scholars have expressed their disappointment at her style in these letters for not matching the excellence of her novel writing. But for us they are glimpses into the private life and self-awareness of an extraordinary woman whose literary achievements are praised the world over.

On friendship
To Fanny Knight, Thursday 20 February 1817
It is very very gratifying to me to know you so intimately. You can hardly think what a pleasure it is to me, to have such thorough pictures of your Heart.

To Cassandra, Monday 24 December 1798
Miss Blanchford is agreeable enough. I do not want people to be very agreeable, as it saves me the trouble of liking them a great deal.

To Cassandra, Sunday 8 February 1807
I am sure I may on this occasion call Kitty Foote . . . 'my very valuable Friend'. Our little visitor has just left us, and left us highly pleased with her; she is a nice, natural, openhearted affectionate girl, with all the ready civility which one sees in the best Children of the present day; so unlike anything that I was myself at her age, that I am often all astonishment and shame.

To Cassandra, Tuesday 12 May 1801
I cannot anyhow continue to find people agreeable; I respect Mrs Chamberlayne for doing her hair well, but cannot feel a more tender sentiment. Miss Langley is like any other short girl with a broad nose and wide mouth, fashionable dress, and exposed bosom.

On housekeeping
To Cassandra, Saturday 17 November 1798
My mother desires for me to tell you that I am a very good housekeeper, which I have no reluctance in doing, because I really think it my peculiar excellence, and for this reason – I always take care to provide such things as please my own appetite, which I consider as chief merit in housekeeping. I have had some ragout veal, and I mean to have some haricot mutton tomorrow. We are to kill a pig soon.

On gossip
To Martha Lloyd, Tuesday 16 February 1893
I suppose all the World is sitting in Judgement upon the Princess of Wales' Letter. Poor woman, I shall support her as long as I can, because she is a Woman, and because I hate her husband – but I can hardly forgive her for calling herself 'attached and affectionate' to a Man whom she must detest – and the intimacy said to subsist between her and Lady Oxford is bad – I do not know what to do about it.

To Cassandra, Monday 20 June 1808
Mr Waller is dead I see; I cannot grieve about it, nor perhaps can his Widow very much.

To Cassandra, Wednesday 29 May 1811
Mrs Harding is a good-looking woman, but not much like Mrs Toke, inasmuch as she is very brown and has scarcely any

teeth; she seems to have some of Mrs Toke's civility but does not profess being so silly.

As an antidote to her propensity for making snide remarks, Jane Austen wrote this personal prayer: Incline us oh God! to think humbly of ourselves, to be severe only in the examination of our own conduct, to consider our fellow-creatures with kindness.

On dancing, dress and diversions
To Cassandra, Monday 24 December 1798
There were twenty dances, and I danced them all, and without any fatigue. I was glad to find myself capable of dancing so much, and with so much satisfaction as I did; from my slender enjoyment of the Ashford balls [as assemblies for dancing] I had not thought myself equal to it, but in cold weather and with few couples I fancy I could just as well dance for a week together as for half an hour.

To Martha Lloyd, Friday 2 September 1814
I am amused by the present style of female dress; the coloured petticoats with braces over the white Spencers and enormous Bonnets upon the full stretch, are quite entertaining.

To Cassandra, Thursday 25 April 1811
I had a pleasant walk in Kensington Gardens on Sunday with Henry – everything was fresh and beautiful. We did go to the play after all on Saturday, we went to the Lyceum, and saw the Hypocrite, an old play taken from Moliere's Tartuffe, and were well entertained.

To Fanny Wright, Thursday 13 March 1817, Chawton
I am got tolerably well again, quite equal to walking about and enjoying the Air. I have a scheme however for accomplishing more, as the weather grows springlike. I mean to take to riding the Donkey. It will be more independent and less troublesome than the use of the carriage.

On her books
To Jane Stanier Clarke, Monday 11 December 1815
My greatest anxiety at present is that this fourth work should not disgrace what was good in the others. But on this point I will do myself the justice to declare that, whatever may be my wishes for its success, I am very strongly haunted with the idea that to those readers who have preferred *Pride and Prejudice*

it will appear inferior in wit, and to those who have preferred *Mansfield Park* very inferior in good sense.

To Cassandra, Thursday 25 April 1811, Sloane St
No indeed, I am never too busy to think of *Sense and Sensibility*. I can no more forget it, than a mother can forget her suckling child, and I am much obliged to you for your enquiries.

To Cassandra, Friday 29 January 1813, Chawton
I want to tell you that I have got my own darling child [*Pride and Prejudice*] from London; on Wednesday I received one copy sent down by Falkner.

A century after Jane Austen's times women found themselves pushed into equality with men by the need to assume the man's role. The Industrial Revolution had brought women into the factories; the two World Wars brought women into men's jobs. This eventuality is delightfully depicted in Jessie Pope's poem which is included in Catherine Reilly's anthology of women's poetry, Scars Upon my Heart.

There's the girl who clips your ticket on the train
  And the girl who speeds the lift from floor to floor,
There's the girl who does a milk-round in the rain,
  And the girl who calls for orders at your door.
  Strong and sensible and fit
  They're out to show their grit,
And tackle jobs with energy and knack.
  No longer caged and penned up
  They're going to keep their end up
Till the khaki soldier boys come marching back.

There's the motor girl who drives a heavy van,
  There's the butcher girl who brings your joint of meat,
There's the girl who cries 'All fares, please!' like a man,
  And the girl who whistles taxis up the street.
  Beneath each uniform
  Beats a heart that's soft and warm,
Though of canny mother-wit they show no lack;
  But a solemn statement this is,
  They've no time for love and kisses
Till the khaki soldier boys come marching back.

Jessie Pope died in 1941. She was a popular contributor to Punch *magazine. Although the 'takeover' she describes was*

Plate 10 Girl of Thetford who is carrying on her father's employment of official Bill poster and Town Crier during the 1914–18 war at work with ladder and paste

temporary, and the boys came marching back, women were never the same again.

Margaret Drabble approaches the issue of working in a man's world with characteristic humour in her first novel, A Summer Bird Cage, *published in 1963. Sarah explains why she will not become a Don*:

'I used to fancy myself as a Don. But I'll tell you what's wrong with that. It's sex. You can't be a sexy Don. It's all right for men being learned and attractive but for women it's a mistake – it detracts from the essential seriousness of the business . . . You'd soon find yourself having to play it down instead of up, if you wanted to get to the top, and when you've only got one life that seems a pity.'

Maude Gonne stood out as an emancipated woman in the 1880s. Her revolutionary spirit harnessed for humanitarian causes was also reflected in her behaviour. Katherine Tynan writes of her in her memories of Dublin at that time:

We were still timidly conventional in Dublin of that day. No woman who was not very emancipated drove on an outside car unaccompanied by a male escort. Miss Gonne drove on a car quite alone, with only her bulldog for escort . . . He followed her once majestically into the dining room of the Westminster Palace Hotel, where she sat at a table at which were a couple of Irish patriots. She was absorbed in conversation when a waiter came and stood respectfully waiting to speak. At last she looked up. Some people in the diningroom had objected to the presence of Madam's bulldog. 'Remove him' said Miss Gonne, with the slightest pause in the conversation. The waiter looked at the bulldog and like a prudent man departed. Presently came the Manager 'Would Madam be good enough to remove her dog?' 'It was entirely against the rules' etc, etc. 'Remove him' said Miss Gonne, proceeding with the conversation. In the result the bulldog stayed.

Virginia Woolf describes the iniquitous and divisive disparities between the sexes in her book Three Guineas, *published in 1938:*

The two classes (men and women) differ enormously. And to

prove this we need not have recourse to the dangerous and uncertain theories of psychologists and biologists, we can appeal to facts. Take the fact of education. Your class has been educated at public schools and universities for five or six hundred years, ours for sixty. Take the fact of property. Your class possesses practically all the capital, all the land, all the valuables, and all the patronage in England. Our class practically none . . . That such differences make for very considerable differences in mind and body, no psychologist or biologist would deny. It would seem to follow, then, as an indisputable factor that 'we' – meaning by 'we' a whole, made up of body, brain and spirit have been so differently trained . . . Though we see the same world, we see it through different eyes.

The feminist movement has attracted criticism for its extreme stance and has been treated somewhat warily by moderate thinkers. Fanny Burney, brought up in the rationalism of the eighteenth century, had a sneaking regard for the feminist attitudes of some of the outstanding women writers of her time. In her last novel, The Wanderer, or Female Difficulties, *published in 1813, she chooses as her principal theme the conflict between the very lady-like heroine, Juliet, and the young revolutionary woman Elinor. Elinor confronts the gentle Juliet:*

'You only fear to alarm, or offend the men – who would keep us from every office but making puddings and pies for their own precious palates! Oh woman, poor subdued woman! thou art as dependent mentally upon the arbitrary customs of man, as man is corporally upon the established laws of his country!'

Mary Hays, an ardent disciple of Mary Wollstonecraft, took up the cause for equality in essays, articles and novels which she wrote in the late eighteenth and early nineteenth century. In this extract from her book Appeal to the Men of Great Britain on behalf of the Women *she pleads for equality:*

You may talk to Woman to eternity of the supreme felicity of pleasing you, though at her own expense, at the expense of her liberty, her property, her natural equality; at the expense of almost every gift with which God may have endowed her, and which you pretend to prune, to garble or to extirpate at will;

I say, you may preach thus to eternity, but you will never convince . . . while the voice of nature pleads within us, and clearly intimates, that a greater degree, a greater proportion of happiness might not be the lot of women if they were allowed, as men are, some vote, some right of judgement in matters which concern them so nearly, as those of the laws and opinions by which they are supposed to be governed. And of which it is but reasonable to suppose that they themselves must be very competent judges.

Elizabeth Barrett Browning expresses similar feelings in her narrative poem 'Aurora Leigh', published in 1856, from which these lines are taken:

You misconceive the question like a man
Who sees the woman as the complement
Of his sex merely. You forget too much
That every creature, female as the male
Stands single in responsible act and thought.
I too have my vocation – work to do,
The heavens and earth have set me.

Celia Fiennes travelled through England, Scotland and Wales in 'a spirit of pure curiosity', recording in a colourful and enthusiastic style everything on the journey that interested her – gardens, architecture, manufacturing, etc. In her journal, Through England on a Side Saddle, *she writes:*

I recommend to all, but especially my own Sex, the study of those things which tend to improve the mind and make our lives pleasant and comfortable as well as profitable in all Stages and Stations of our Lives, and render Suffering and Age supportable and Death less formidable and a future Stage more happy.

A charming example of Celia Fiennes' writing is her description of taking a bathe in the Cross Baths at Bath in or before 1687 – from The Journey of Celia Fiennes*:*

The ladyes goes into the bath with garments made of fine yellow canvas which is stiff and made large with great sleeves, like a parson's gown, the water fills it up so that it's borne off that your shape is not seen, it does not cling close as other linning which looks sadly in the poorer sort that go in their own linning. When you go out of the bath you go within a door that leads to steps which you ascend by degrees . . . so you are in a private place, and let your canvass drop off by degrees into the water, which your woman guide takes off and in the mean tyme your maide flings a garment of flanell made like as night-gown with great sleeves over your head, and the guides take the taile and so put it on you just as you rise the steps and your other garment drops off so you are wrapped up in the flannell and your nightgown the top, your slippers, and so you are set in a Chaire; the chaires are a low seate and with frames around and over your head and all covered inside and out with red bayes and a curtain drawn before of the same which makes it close and warm; then a couple of men with staves takes and carryes you to your lodging and sets you at your bedside where you go to bed and lay and sweat sometyme as you please; your maide and the maides of the house gets your fire and waites on you till you rise to get out of your sweat.

Mrs Elizabeth Elsted, born in 1683, was the first woman to study the Anglo-Saxon language. She was a great scholar – a true 'Blue Stocking' – translating and commenting upon the collection of English Saxon Homilies of Alfric, Archbishop of Canterbury. In her edition of the Homily on the birthday of St Gregory, which appeared in 1709, she sets out to answer the question 'What has a woman to do with learning?'

For my part I could never think any part of Learning either useless, or contemptible, because I knew not the Advantages of it; I have rather thought myself obliged to reverence those who are skilful in any Art or Profession, and can gladly subscribe to the Praise of any liberal Accomplishment, be it in any Person, of any Sex.

Hannah Wolley was a professional teacher in the mid-seventeenth century. She was active in the early stages of English feminism. Besides teaching, she brought up a large family and wrote several books. In the preface to her best-known book, The Gentlewoman's Companion, *she wrote:*

The right education of the female sex, as it is in a manner everywhere neglected, so it ought to be generally lamented. Most in this depraved later Age think a woman learned enough if she can distinguish her Husband's bed from another's . . . I cannot but complain of, and must condemn the great negligence of Parents, in letting the fertile ground of their daughters lie fallow, yet send the barren Noodles of their sons to the University, where they stay for no purpose than to fill their empty sconces with idle notions.

It was not until centuries later that women could aspire to a university education. Dorothy L. Sayers, famous for her detective novels, translations and religious plays, was one of the women to do so. The following passage is taken from an address she gave in 1938 under the title 'Are Women Human?':

'When the pioneers of university training for women demanded that women should be admitted to the universities, the cry went up at once, 'Why should women want to know about Aristotle?' The answer is NOT that all women would be better for knowing about Aristotle but simply 'What women want as a class is irrelevant. I want to know about Aristotle. It is true that many women care nothing about him and a great many male undergraduates turn pale and faint at the thought of him. But I – eccentric individual that I am – do want to know about Aristotle and I submit that there is nothing in my shape or bodily functions which need prevent my knowing about him.'

A great deal of reform was necessary before women could go to the universities to finish their education. Josephine Kamm's book How Different from Us *is devoted to the story of Dorothea Beale and Frances Buss whom she describes as 'the last of the distinguished band of reformers who had unlocked the doors of education to future generations of women'. Dorothea Beale was elected Principal of Cheltenham Ladies College in 1858 and remained there for nearly fifty years. Frances Buss became Headmistress of the North London Collegiate School. They both founded teacher training and university colleges for women, and improved education for girls from families of a lower income bracket. In a lighter vein, they both inspired two anonymous rhymesters to compose these verses:*

Plate 11 The first five students of Girton College Cambridge, 1874

Said Miss Beale to Miss Buss,
'There is no one like us.'
Said Miss Buss to Miss Beale
'That is just what I feel.'

Miss Buss and Miss Beale
Cupid's darts do not feel,
They leave that to us,
Poor Miss Beale and Miss Buss.

In this climate of educational reform, George Eliot was writing, in 1856, about the place of knowledge in the life of 'the cultured woman':

The really cultured woman is all the simpler and the less obtrusive for her knowledge . . . she does not make it a pedestal from which she flatters herself that she commands a complete view of men and things, but makes it a point of observation from which to form a right estimate of herself. She neither spouts poetry nor quotes Cicero on slight provocation. She does not write books to confound philosophers, perhaps because she is able to write books to delight them. In conversation she is the least formidable of women, because she understands that you can't understand her.

George Eliot refrained from political involvement in the women's suffrage movement, although she approved of feminism in theory.

Harriet Martineau, who was working in the middle of the nineteenth century as a self-taught and very successful political journalist, made these comments on the emerging Women's Rights movement:

Nobody can be further than I am from being satisfied with the condition of my own sex, under law and custom of my own country; but I decline all fellowship and cooperation with women of genius or otherwise favourable position, who injure the cause by their personal tendencies. When I see an eloquent writer insinuating to everybody who comes across her that she is the victim of her husband's carelessness and cruelty, while he never spoke in his own defence: when I see her violating all good taste by her obtrusiveness in society and oppressing everybody about her with her epicurean selfishness every day, while raising in print an eloquent cry on behalf of the oppressed: I feel to the bottom of my heart that she is the worst enemy of the cause she professes to plead.

There were others who had achieved great advances for the causes of women, whose approval was not forthcoming and who queried the aims and accomplishments of the Feminist movements. Eleanor Rathbone, a member of the National Union of Societies for Equal Citizenship, conducted an assault in the late 1920s on what she called the 'me too feminism'. She said:

'The habit of continually measuring women's wants by men's achievements seems out of date, ignominious and intolerably boring'.

Other women with queries are Florence Nightingale: 'There are evils which press more hardly on women than the want of suffrage'; and Mrs Beatrice Webb: 'At the root of my anti-feminism lay the fact that I had never suffered the disabilities assumed to arise from my sex'.

Rosamund Lehmann gives an indication of the confusion and uncertainty that changes in women's circumstances have brought with them. She expresses her feelings through her heroine Dinah at the end of her novel The Echoing Grove, *published in 1953:*

'I can't help thinking it's particularly difficult to be a woman at present. One feels so transitional and fluctuating . . . so I suppose do men. I believe we are all in flux – that the difference between our grandmothers and us is far deeper than we realise – much more fundamental than the obvious social economic one. Our so-called emancipation may be a symptom, not a cause. Sometimes I think it's more than the development of a new attitude towards sex: that a new gender may be evolving – psychically new – a sort of hybrid. Or else it's just beginning to be uncovered – how much woman there is in man and vice versa.'

Plate 12 'Blest with a second race, the Grandma shares, the fond reward of her maternal cares'
Etching by Maria Cosway, 1800

4

In old age

What has become of those images of hope and innocence, fearlessness and fervour, aspiration and endeavour? What glimpses do we get of woman in her final years hampered by physical and mental debility, and our century's added scourge, an old age stripped of dignity? Around us we see grandmothers wasted of their matriarchal role as families disband and scatter; in their old age demeaned by media which would show us youth is all and all is for youth.

Our appreciation of old THINGS is growing. We surround ourselves with period pieces and masterpieces; we wear down the flagstones of our mansions and museums in search of heritage. Can this be a prelude to our restoring respect, usefulness and glory to old age and to our reappraisal of the wisdom of experience in ageing minds? If woman could find ways to integrate the old into our society: to make the attainment of age once more a source of pride, what splendid new images of achievement we would have!

Images of beauty and blessings in old age seem rare. We condition ourselves to dread the ageing process from the onset of middle age, the menopause, and the first appearance of wrinkles. But beauty there is and blessings there are. Virginia Woolf gives us a sensitive description of an older woman's beauty in her major novel To The Lighthouse, *published in 1927:*

. . . and all at once he realised that it was this: it was this:- she was the most beautiful person he had ever seen.

With stars in her eyes and veils in her hair, with cyclamen and wild violets – what nonsense was he thinking? She was fifty at least; she had eight children. Stepping through fields of flowers and taking to her breast buds that had broken and lambs that had fallen; with the stars in her eyes and the wind in her hair . . .

'But she's no more aware of her beauty than a child.' . . . For always, he thought, there was something incongruous to be worked into the harmony of her face. She clapped a deer-stalker's hat on her head; she ran across the lawn in goloshes to snatch a child from mischief. So that if it were her beauty merely that one thought of, one must remember the quivering thing, the living thing, . . . and work it into the picture; or if one thought of her simply as a woman, one must endow her with some freak of idiosyncrasy; or suppose some latent desire to doff her royalty of form as if her beauty bored her and all that men say of beauty, and she wanted only to be like other people, insignificant.

Sexagenarians can take heart from Jane Digby's experience. She was successively Lady Ellenborough, Baroness Venningen, Countess Theotky and the wife of the Shikh Abdul Medjuel El Mezrab. On her birthday in 1869, Jane Digby el Mezrab wrote: 'Sixty-two years of age, and an impetuous girl of seventeen cannot exceed me in ardent passionate feelings'. Two years earlier Mrs Isabel Burton, wife of the great orientalist Richard Burton, visited Jane Digby in Damascus and recalls in her memoirs her impressions of this great romantic and adventuress:

She was a most beautiful woman, though at the time I write she was 61, tall, commanding and queen-like. She was *la grande dame au bout des doigts*, as much as if she had just left the salons of London and Paris, refined in manner and voice, nor did she ever utter a word you could wish unsaid. My husband thought she was out and out the cleverest woman he ever met; there was nothing she could not do. She spoke nine languages perfectly and could read and write in them. Her letters were splendid; if on business there was never a word too much, nor a word too little. She had a most romantic adventurous life, and she was now, one might say, Lady Hester Stanhope's successor.

When I first saw her in Damascus she led a semi-European life.

She blackened her eyes with kohl, and lived in a curiously untidy manner. But otherwise she was not in the least extraordinary. She was honoured and respected as queen of her tribe, wearing one blue garment, her beautiful hair in two long plaits down to the ground, milking the camels, serving her husband, preparing his food, giving him water to wash his hands and face, sitting on the floor washing his feet, giving him his coffee, his sherbet, his narghilyes, and while he ate she stood and waited on him and glorying in it. She looked splended in oriental dress, and if you saw her in the bazaar you would have said she was not more than 54 years of age.

Dame Rose Macaulay describes woman plotting her life in stages of seven years. This excerpt is from a letter written to her sister on 24 March 1929:

Dearest Jeanie,

I am just back from Petersfield, and keeping Margaret's birthday. We read the poem about 'Seven Times' ['Songs of Seven' by Jean Ingelow, 1820–1897] as she was 7 times 7 today, but the lady in the poem had been very unfortunate and she had lost her husband and all her children and was bewailing an empty nest and looking towards her end. M. is luckier. But I always thought that woman had a discontented nature. She was happy at 7 x 1, but at 7 x 2 was pinning all her hopes on the future instead of enjoying her birthday; she was tolerably cheerful (being excited by love) at 7 x 3, but more or less worried by 7 x 4, and a miserable widow at 7 x 5, and 7 x 6, when she was getting a daughter married, she could only think how she had given up all and was now losing her child and getting no thanks . . .

Rose Macaulay, novelist and journalist, won many literary awards. She was a prolific letter writer and her lifelong correspondence with her sister has been bound into a volume, Letters to a Sister, *published in 1964.*

Doris Lessing gives us a description of a middle-aged woman experiencing an all too common feeling of redundancy, in Summer Before the Dark, *published in 1973:*

The small, chill wind was blowing definitely, if still softly enough, this was the first time in her life that Kate was not wanted. She was unnecessary. That this time in her life was approaching she had of course known very well for years. She had even made plans for it; she would study this, travel there, take up this or that type of welfare work. It is not possible, after all, to be a woman with any sort of a mind, and not know that in middle age, in the full flood of one's capacities and energies one is bound to become that well-documented and much studied phenomenon, the woman with grown-up children and not enough to do, whose energies must be switched from the said children to less vulnerable targets, for everybody's sake, her own as well as theirs. So there was nothing surprising about what was happening. Perhaps she ought to have expected it sooner.

She had not expected it this summer. Next summer, or the year after that, yes, but not now. What she had set herself to face had been all in the future. But it was now that it was happening.

George Eliot considered herself middle-aged at thirty-eight when, on the last night of 1857, she wrote these encouraging lines:

My life has deepened unspeakably during the last year. I feel a greater capacity for moral and intellectual enjoyment; a more acute sense of my deficiencies in the past, a more solemn desire to be faithful to coming duties, than I remember at any former period of my life. And my happiness has deepened too; the blessedness of perfect love and union growing daily . . . Few women, I fear, have had such reason as I have, to think the long, sad years of youth were worth living for the sake of middle age.

The beauty that comes from singularity and distinction is often attached to those of more advanced years. One such picture comes from Mrs Edward Montagu, writing in 1762 of her relation, Lady Mary Wortley Montagu, who was seventy-three years old and who had recently returned to England after living abroad for thirty-five years.

When Nature is at the trouble of making a very singular person, Time does right in respecting it. Medals are preserved when common coin is worn out; and as great geniuses are rather matters of curiosity than of art, this lady seems reserved to be a wonder for more than our generation. She does not look older than when she went abroad, has more than the vivacity of fifteen, and a memory which perhaps is unique . . . I visited her because her cousin and mine were cousins German. Tho' she has not any foolish partiality for her husband or his relations, I was very graciously received and you may imagine entertained by one who neither thinks, speaks, acts nor dresses like anybody else.

In the following passages, three grand-daughters look back at three old ladies who had charm, dignity, generosity, and obviously much affection. Katherine Mansfield wrote this of her grandmother in her diary in 1922:

Grandma's birthday. Where is that photograph of my dear love leaning against her husband's shoulder with her hair parted so meekly and her eyes raised? I love it. I long to have it. For one thing, Mother gave it to me at a time when she loved me . . . But for another – so much more important, it is she, my own Grandma, young and lovely. That arm. That baby's sleeve with the velvet ribbon. I must see them again.

And one day I must write about Grandma at length, especially of her beauty in her bath – when she was about sixty, wiping herself with the towel. I remember how lovely she seemed to me. And her fine linen, her throat, her scent. I have never really described her yet. Patience – the time will come.

Many of Katherine Mansfield's short stories are drawn from her childhood in New Zealand before she came to England to establish herself as an innovative writer.

In her autobiography, My First Hundred Years, *archaeologist Margaret Murray describes her paternal grandmother:*

Grandmother Phoebe Murray was already over sixty when I first remember her. She was always dainty in her dress and dignified in manner. She never read anything but her Bible and prayer-book and the newspaper (omitting all politics). I never heard her say an unkind or catty thing about anyone, none of her family could do wrong in her eyes, she was generous as far as her means would allow, she had great charm of manner, and she had the faculty of driving one mad from sheer exasperation.

One might say that she fussed, but lots of people are fussy without being exasperating. I think she thought that the way to show real affection was to imagine dangers and then to try to protect the loved ones by perpetual warnings, and by a perpetual desire to see them, if they were doing anything unusual, so as to make sure they were not dead.

Gwen Raverat, writing in 1952 in her autobiographical Period Piece, *remembers a delightful octogenarian:*

After nursery breakfast we always began by paying a round of calls on the people who were having breakfast in bed. First of all we went to see Grandmama and her little fox terrier Dicky. Grandmama was now a very old lady; she was over eighty before I can remember her and she always went out in a Bath chair. I liked her very much indeed. We used to play on her bed with little tin pots and pans, called Pottikins and Pannikins, and then she gave us bits of liquorice out of her work basket, cut up with her work scissors. I don't think the work basket was ever used for anything but liquorice, which she kept for her cough. Indeed, I have the basket itself still and it contains nothing but some half-finished book markers, worked in cross stitch by my uncles Leonard and Horace – her little boys – in the Fifties of the last century.

Period Piece *describes Gwen Raverat's childhood in Cambridge as daughter of a Cambridge University Professor. She became a member of the Society of Wood Engravers and was known for her book and anthology illustrations.*

Some find it good to take stock, to look back, to give thanks. For them, like Agatha Christie, to remember is a blessing:

So many other things to remember: walking up through a carpet of flowers to the Yezidi shrine at Sheikh Adi . . . the beauty of the great tiled mosque of Isfahan – a fairy story city . . . a red sunset outside the house at Nimrud . . . getting out of the New Forest in autumn . . . swimming in the sea in Torbay with Rosalind . . . Matthew playing in the Eton and

Harrow match . . . Max arriving home from the war and eating kippers with me . . . So many things – some silly, some funny, some beautiful.

A child says 'Thank God for my good dinner.' What can I say at 75? 'Thank God for my good life, and for all the love that has been given to me.'

So wrote the 'Queen of Crime' in the epilogue to her autobiography, published a year after her death in 1977. During her lifetime she wrote seventy-seven detective novels and books of stories which have been translated into every major language and whose copies run into tens of millions.

Blanch Parry looks back on her lifetime spent at court in service to Queen Elizabeth 1. She died on 12 February 1589 in her eighty-second year. This poem is her inscription:

I lived always as handmaid to a Queen,
In chamber chief my time did overpass
Uncareful of my wealth there was I seen,
Whilst I abode the running of my glass,
Not doubting want whilst that my mistress lived,
In woman's state whose cradle saw I rocked,
Her servant then, as when she her crown achieved,
And so remained till death he my door had knocked . . .
So that my time I thus did pass away,
A maid in court, and never no man's wife
Sworn of Queen Ellspeth's head chamber always,
With Maiden Queen a maid did end my life.

Dorothy Richardson sees this 're-realisation' of one's life in old age in a particularly original way. Towards the end of her life, in 1957, she wrote to a friend:

Old age offers compensations. For side by side with loss are gains that take one by surprise. For one thing, with relatively nothing ahead, one comes in, so to speak, to all one's investments . . . the whole of one's life, finished and complete, comes into one's hands for re-realisation. And this past, sometimes described as reared up and staring one in the face, is misrepresented in being called 'unalterable'.

Dorothy Richardson's works have inspired many of our best twentieth-century writers, and her life is an example to all women who seek to follow a path of their own.

Enid Bagnold sets at the centre of her play 'The Chinese Prime Minister' a woman who, at seventy, intends to live for herself, to realise the 'ME' in her. In justifying the play to Dame Edith Evans in 1963, Ms Bagnold wrote:

It's not the size of the subject that matters. In this play I write of a woman who, having experienced all womanhood, love, passion, birth, marriage, motherhood, grandmotherhood, exclaims 'I have never conquered the ME in me and don't intend to! Without it nothing has importance!' She is seventy. She intends to be done with her loves, her time-table, her domestic harness, and stand up like a rock alone and look out with her eyes over the last sea. She sheds 'woman' – as a snake casts its fine silver skin. Who else but I could have written it? Because this is how I feel. This is an honest play that is written out of an honest heart. This woman isn't playing grandmother – playing cosy – playing abdication. If I am not to live for myself NOW – she says – after three score years and ten – then when can I do it?

Enid Bagnold was responding to the criticism from Dame Edith of the play being about 'a group of selfish people when there's Cuba and the Bomb to worry about'. Their correspondence is recorded in Bryan Forbes' biography of Dame Edith entitled Ned's Girl.

Many women approach old age in the same positive way that they have met every other challenge in their lives. They give us images of hope and encouragement. At the age of sixty-four, in 1944, Marie Stopes, the indefatigable birth control pioneer, wrote this poem 'To The Old':

Weep from your depths no drizzling red-eyed tears
Nor wail within a house of shuttered doors;
Do not thus slay young hope with your harsh years
Nor petrify our quickened hearts with yours.
Age nobly! Clad in velvet bloom, and shine
Upon life's banquet with creative eyes;
Rise every morning making each day fine,

Lead grandly homeward to serener skies.
  Youth has its joys, but rapture of the soul
  Grows with sweet age as life nears heaven, its goal.

Marie Stopes died in 1958 at the age of seventy-eight. She spent her life trying to combat sexual ignorance in women, and haphazard reproduction.

In 1896, Florence Nightingale had a legendary nursing career behind her, and to her credit many articles and books which did much to improve all aspects of medical work at home and abroad. She had settled in London, living the retired life of a semi-invalid, but still active in mind – and pen. She inaugurated funds for the purpose of founding a training school for nurses which was subsequently opened in 1860 at St Thomas' Hospital in London. At the age of seventy-six, and having achieved so much, she could still write in her diary:

There is so much to live for. I have lost much in failures and disappointments as well as in grief. Do you know, life is more precious to me now in my old age. Yes, one does feel the passing away of so many who seemed essential to the world. I have none now to whom I could speak of those who are gone. But all the more I am eager to see successors. I thank God for having given me work, constant work. I wish no memorial whatever to mark the place where lies my mortal soul but that I should be carried to the nearest convenient burial ground accompanied by no more than two persons without trappings – after that my body has been given for dissection or post mortem examination for the purposes of medical science.

This passage raises one of the saddest aspects of old age – the passing away of so many who seemed essential to the world. For with the loss of each valuable friend, that part of one which lived only in their existence also dies.

Cassandra Austen expresses this in a letter to Fanny Knight in July 1817, on the death of her sister Jane Austen:

I have lost a treasure, such a sister, such a friend as never can have been surpassed. She was the sun of my life, the gilder of every pleasure, the soother of every sorrow. I had not concealed a thought from her, and it is as if I had lost part of myself. I loved her only too well.

I thank God that I was enabled to attend her to the last and amongst my many causes of self reproach I have not to add any wilful neglect of her comfort.

When I asked her if there was anything she wanted she answered, 'Nothing but Death'.

Queen Victoria never recovered from the early death of her beloved Prince Albert. Although she lived to the age of eighty-two, she spoke of being in her old age when she was but forty-six. A year earlier, in 1865, she wrote about her loss in a letter, published in Letters to my Daughter*:*

I have been daily on my pony wandering quietly among the splendid fresh, green foliage, which is now very forward, all the oaks being out since a week! The birds sing . . . all lovely, but all bereft of joy, for he is not on earth to enjoy it with me as he did.

I always feel – when I wander about, so kindly cared for and able to have all I can wish for, and yet without joy, that it is like a pilgrimage! Soothing, as all breathes of him – but terribly joyless. But when I'm out I can rest and I can think Darling Papa is 'out' too. It is the return home with that silent room nearby and fagged to death with work which is fearful indeed.

Isabel Burton felt as passionately towards her husband in death as she had done during his lifetime. Richard Burton, famous traveller and orientalist, died in 1890 and their story is recorded in Lesley Blanche's book The Wilder Shores of Love, *from which we learn of Isabel's remark to a friend:*

Do not be so hard and prosaic as to suppose that the dead cannot, in rare instances, come back and tell us how it is with them. I talk with my darling nearly every day.

Other images of sadness there are in old age. Edith Sitwell writes some of them in a poem published in 1945 when she was fifty-eight. This is part of that poem, 'The Poet Laments the Coming of Old Age':

In old age

I see the children running out of school;
They are taught that Goodness means a blinding hood
Or is heaped by Time like the hump on an aged back,
And that Evil can be cast like an old rag
and Wisdom caught like a hare and held in the golden sack
Of the heart . . .
. . . But Goodness grew not with age, although my heart must bear
The weight of all Time's filth, and Wisdom is not a hare in the golden sack
Of the heart . . . It can never be caught. Though I bring back sight to the blind
My seed of Folly has gone, that could teach me to bear
That the gold-sinewed body that had the blood of all the earth in its veins
Has changed to an old rag of the outworn world
And the great heart that the first Morning made
Should wear all Time's destruction for a dress.

Dame Edith Sitwell's poetry, her voice, her face of extraordinary beauty, her extravagant dress and her eccentric way of life, enriched English cultural life until her death at the age of seventy-seven in 1964. Fortunately many recordings of her reading her own poetry remain, the most famous being her reading of 'Facade' to the music of Sir William Walton.

Alice Meynell sees old age as 'the mournful plain where thou must wander'. Here is her poem 'A Letter from a Girl to Her Own Old Age'. Alice Meynell was poet, essayist and active suffragette. She died at the age of seventy-five in 1922 having published numerous articles and anthologies as well as having raised a family of eight children. Her husband was the author Wilfred Meynell.

Listen, and when thy hand this paper presses,
O time-worn woman, think of her who blesses
What thy thin fingers touch, with her caresses.

O mother, for the weight of years that break thee!
O daughter, for slow Time must yet awake thee,
And from the changes of my heart must make thee.

Plate 13 'Old woman and girl' by J M Cameron, 186–

In old age

O fainting traveller, morn is grey in heaven.
Dost thou remember how the clouds were driven?
And are they calm about the fall of even?

Pause near the ending of thy long migration,
For this one sudden hour of desolation
Appeals to one hour of thy meditation.

Suffer, O silent one, that I remind thee
Of the great hills that stormed the sky behind thee
Of the wild winds of power that have resigned thee.

Know that the mournful plain where thou must wander
Is but a grey and silent world, but ponder
The misty mountains of the morning yonder.

Listen:- the mountain winds with rain were fretting,
And sudden gleams the mountain-tops besetting.
I cannot let thee fade to death, forgetting.

What part of this wild heart of mine I know not
Will follow with thee where the great winds blow not
And where the young flowers of the mountain grow not.

I have not writ this letter divining
To make a glory of thy silent pining,
A triumph of thy mute and strange declining.

Only one youth, and the bright life is shrouded,
Only one morning, and the day was clouded.
And one old age with all regrets is crowded.

O hush, O hush! Thy fears my words are steeping.
O hush, hush, hush! So full, the faint of weeping?
Poor eyes, so quickly moved, so near to sleeping?

Pardon the girl; such strange desires beset her.
Poor woman, lay aside the mournful letter
That breaks thy heart; the one who wrote, forget her:

The one who now thy faded features guesses
With filial fingers thy grey hair caresses,
With morning tears thy mournful twilight blesses.

Virginia Woolf shows a sensitive perception of the debility of age and the tenacity of the character of Mrs Grey in Old Mrs Grey, *published posthumously in 1942:*

Mrs Grey sat on a hard chair in the corner looking – but at what? Apparently at nothing. She did not change the focus of her eyes when visitors came in. Her eyes had ceased to focus themselves; it may be that they had lost their power. They were aged eyes, blue unspectacled. They could see, but without looking. She had never used her eyes on anything minute and difficult, merely upon faces and dishes and fields. And now at the age of 92, they saw nothing but a zigzag of pain. Her body was wrapped round the pain as a damp sheet is folded over a wire.

'My brothers and sisters and my husband gone,' she mumbled. 'My daughter too. But I go on. Every morning I pray God to let me pass.'

'The doctor comes every week, he's a good man. He says he wonders I don't go, my heart's all wind and water. Yet I don't seem able to die.'

So we, humanity, insist that the body still cling to the wire. We pinion it there with a bottle of medicine, a cup of tea, a dying fire, like a rook on a barn door, but a rook that still lives even with a nail through it.

Virginia Woolf died at the age of fifty-nine having endured much mental suffering and ill health during her nonetheless intensely creative life.

Old age was a struggle, too, for actress Mrs Patrick Campbell who, in 1927, at the age of sixty-two, had squandered two fortunes and was finding it hard to make ends meet. She wrote to George Bernard Shaw:

I was under the impression that the great battle of life was fought in our youth, – not a bit of it – it's when we are old, and our work not wanted, that it rages and goes on – and on – and on.

Many cope with old age by simply not acknowledging it. We are told that age is just a state of mind. Fanny Burney gives us a picture of Mrs Mittin in Camilla, *published in 1796, and her endeavours to disguise her age and celibacy:*

'Well now, young ladies . . . I'm going to tell you a secret. Do you know, for all I call myself Mrs., I'm single.'

'Dear La,' exclaimed Miss Dennel. 'And for all you're so old!'

'So old, Miss! Who told you I was so old? I'm not so very old as you may think me. I'm no particular age, I assure you. Why, what made you think of that?'

'La, I don't know. Only you don't look very young.'

'I can't help that, Miss Dennel. Perhaps you mayn't look young yourself one of these days. People can't always stand still just at a particular minute. Why, how old now do you take me to be? Come, be sincere.'

'La, I'm sure I can't tell; only I thought you was an old woman.'

'An old woman! Lord, my dear, people would laugh to hear you. You don't know what an old woman is. Why, it's being a cripple, and blind, and deaf, and dumb, and slavering, and without a tooth. Pray, how am I like all that?'

'Nay, I'm sure I don't know. Only I thought by the look of your face, you must be monstrous old.'

'Lord, I can't think what you've got in your poor head, Miss Dennel. I never heard as much before, since I was born. Why, the reason I'm called Mrs. is not because of that, I assure you. But because I'd a mind to be taken for a young widow on account that everybody likes a young widow and if one is called Miss people begin soon to think one an old maid, that it's quite disagreeable.'

Acceptance of old age and a coming to terms with it give us some pleasing images. Among these are the eccentric old ladies who get the very most out of life to the last. Margaret Thompson is described by Catherine Caulfield in The Emperor of the United States of America and other Magnificent British Eccentrics, *published in 1981:*

Margaret Thompson was first and foremost a lover of snuff. So strong was her fondness for this substance that when she died in 1776 she left instructions in her will that in the coffin her body be completely covered with the best Scotch snuff instead of flowers, since 'nothing can be so fragrant and refreshing to me as that precious powder'. As a preliminary to this she directed her maid, Sarah Stuart, should line the coffin with all Miss Thompson's unwashed handkerchiefs.

No man was allowed to approach the open casket, but once closed it was carried by six men – the greatest snuff-takers in the parish of St James, Westminster, wearing snuff-coloured beaver hats rather than ordinary mourning clothes, and six old maids wearing hoods and carrying a box of snuff as they went along.

The funeral procession was led by the minister, whom Miss Thompson desired to take on the way a certain quantity of the said snuff, not exceeding one pound. Sarah Stuart walked alongside him tossing large handfuls of the snuff to the crowds who followed behind. For those who did not attend the funeral, Miss Thompson left orders that two bushels of snuff be given away afterwards at her house.

Dame Edith Sitwell maintained that eccentricity 'exists particularly in the English, and partly I think because of that peculiar and satisfactory knowledge of infallibility that is the hallmark and birthright of the British nation'. In her book The English Eccentrics *she recalls:*

'Lady' Lawson (born in 1700) lived in Coldbath Square, Clerkenwell, for ninety years . . . she never washed herself for fear of catching cold, and so laying the foundation of a disease. She does, however, besmear herself with hog's lard, to which she adds rose-pink over the cheeks.

This strange antique trumpery, at the age of eighty seven, cut two new teeth, which were a source of pride to her and of wonder to her neighbours.

Her large house in Coldbath Square contains only four other beings, ghosts like herself, two old lap-dogs, an aged cat and an old man who 'Lady' Lawson has taken into her house where he acts as steward, butler, cook and housemaid.

The house was large it seems and elegantly furnished. The beds were made every day, as if visitors were expected, though nobody ever came. As for 'Lady' Lawson's room, it was never washed and only swept very occasionally, whilst the windows were so crusted with dirt that they hardly admitted a ray of light. For 'Lady' Lawson believed that a drop of water in her room would be as dangerous as the sea.

She would sit and read, or talk of events of the last hundred years to the few acquaintances whom she permitted to visit her . . . The immortality of this old lady seemed assured, until the sudden death of an ancient neighbour caused her to tremble – to doubt in her own immortality. She weakened, took to her bed, and on Tuesday the 28th May died at the age of One Hundred and Sixteen Years.

Muriel Spark devoted her novel Memento Mori, *published in 1959, to elderly characters. This one had a most amusing idea:*

Lisa Brooke died in her 73rd year after a second stroke. She had taken nine months to die and in fact it was only one year before her death that feeling rather ill she had decided to reform her life, and reminding herself how attractive she still was, offered up the new idea – celibacy, to the Lord, to whom no gift whatsoever is unacceptable.

Mother Stewart, an old travelling saleswoman, appears in Harriet Martineau's book A Guide to the Lakes or Life in the Lake District, *published in 1850.*

We are stopped at the gate by Mother Stewart, looks so weather-beaten today as to show that she has only just arrived from peregrination and here comes her cart, with her son in it, driving slowly, that he may not break my new crockery . . . How gipsy-like she looks, with her red and blue handkerchief hanging about her face under her weather-beaten black bonnet, and her arms akimbo except when she takes her pipe from her mouth to speak! When her ware is all spread out on the kitchen floor, I see how good her taste is and I praise the chamber-ewers and basins, the water pitchers and tea service . . . She wants my opinion what to do with her young daughter who is subject to fits. She finds no good effect from what was affirmed to her would be a cure – binding the backbones of three sprats upon the girl's breast when she went to bed. When her wares are checked off by the list, and I have put a pen in her hand, big hand that she may make her mark, Mrs Stewart ties up her money in a bag and gives me her last, affectionate nod, resumes her pipe, and leaves us to prosecute our walk.

Beatrix Potter describes an old character in her journal in 1894 while staying in Scotland:

I met an old woman down by the river Tweed, gathering sticks in a sack. She is often there smoking a pipe, no teeth, rather good features and sharp eyes. A regular old witch.

After some remarks she said there was not enough water and that when there was – 'they' came to the edge. Thinking she meant driftwood I sympathised and presently discovered that 'they' meant salmon. I never met such a sinful old poacher, I don't know when I laughed so. Scorning to tell a lie she said she could take them out with a crook, put them in her poke, her skirt turned up, or in her sack. 'They can't punish a woman for poaching you know.' Which I take to be Berwick law. She said it with such a sly twinkle I thought she might be crazy, but there was very shrewd method in her madness, and she ended in begging for a petticoat which I was sorry I could not bestow in return for this entertainment.

Mrs Ann Radcliffe gives us this picture of a woman experiencing the dying of the year in the autumn of her life. The passage is taken from her book The Mysteries of Udolpho, *published in 1794. It sets the scene for the final stage of life:*

It was a grey autumnal evening towards the close of the season; heavy mists and a chilling breeze that sighed among the beech-woods, strewed her path with some of their last yellow leaves. These circling in the blast and foretelling the death of the year, gave an image of desolation to her mind.

She walked mournfully on, watching the swallows tossed along the wind, the afflictions and vicissitudes of her late life seemed portrayed in these fleeting images.

Old age brings with it a capacity to look beyond, to contemplate what might come next. The spiritual world comes sharply into focus. In the nineteenth century particularly, hymns were one of the few means of expression open to women as an outlet for their thoughts and feelings on this subject. Hymn writing was a traditional and acceptable outlet provided by the Church of England for women with poetic gifts and Christian faith to use their talents. No less than thirty women contributed to the

English Hymnal, and some of the hymns they wrote are still among the most popular for Morning Service and Evensong – hymns such as 'There is a Green Hill Far Away', by Mrs C. F. Alexander; 'Oh Perfect Love, all Human Thought Transcending', by Mrs Dorothy Frances Guerney; and this hymn by Sarah Adam which discloses her spiritual fervour as she approached the end of her life in 1848:

Nearer, my God, to Thee,
  Nearer to Thee!
E'en though it be a cross
  That raiseth me
Still all my song would be,
Nearer, my God, to Thee,
  Nearer to Thee!

Though like the wanderer
  The sun gone down,
Darkness be over me,
  My rest a stone
Yet in my dreams I'd be
Nearer, my God, to Thee,
  Nearer to Thee!

There let the way appear,
  Steps unto heaven;
All that Thou send'st to me
  In mercy given.
Angels to beckon me
Nearer, my God, to Thee,
  Nearer to Thee!

Dame Edith Sitwell, whom we saw lamenting the onset of old age, still searched for 'a rebirth of faith and wonder'. These were the opening lines of her 'Invocation' from 'Green Song', published in 1944:

I who was once a golden woman like those who walk
In the dark heavens – but am now grown old
And sit by the fire, and see the fire grow cold,
Watch the dark fields for a rebirth of faith and wonder.

Dame Edith Sitwell's contemporary, Dame Sybil Thorndike (1882–1976), also had hopes of a future life, as we see in this extract from Sheridan Morley's biography Sybil Thorndike, A Life in the Theatre. *She was asked, on her ninetieth birthday, if she had regrets. Her response shows a grand acceptance of her condition:*

'Not many: sometimes I wish I didn't have such a temper, and I wish Lewis and I hadn't had to quarrel so dreadfully, but then again I think that was so much a part of us and our marriage that we couldn't have lived any other way . . . I regret the pain I'm in now, with this bally arthritis, and I wish I were strong enough to make it go away, and I get so cross that I can't do much, but I've had a very long and healthy life so I can't really complain, now can I? Though of course I do.'

'I suppose I regret the way the theatre has changed, the way that actors nowadays mumble and you can't often hear a word they say, but I can still hear Gielgud and Richardson and Larry and they should be enough for anyone.'

'I find I dream a lot more than I used to, usually about a place near the sea where there are great rocks and there's a long stretch of sand: whenever I have that dream Lewis is always standing there, so I hope perhaps that's where we're going in another life.'

Margaret Murray was an archaeologist and Egyptologist. Her writings and lectures on folklore and anthropology were influential contributions to British scholarship. Her autobiography, My First Hundred Years, *published in 1963, shows her very confident attitude towards death:*

This is the faith in which I face the coming of that passing into the unknown which we call Death. It is that to each human soul there is given a piece of work to do with the choice to accept or refuse. If accepted and carried out to the best of one's ability the reward will be a removal to some higher sphere of activity and responsibility. If refused, and the soul chooses to go its own wilful way, it returns again and again until the lesson is learned. It is my firm belief that, though the physical body may change and decay, and fear disunion which we call Death, yet the mind and soul of each individual passes on to some higher knowledge, some closer approach to that Almighty Power, in which we live, and move and have our being.

Actress Fanny Kemble, who died in her eighties in 1893, sought immortality:

Let me not die for ever, when I'm gone
  To the cold earth: but let my memory
Live like the gorgeous, Western light that shone
  Over the clouds where sunk day's majesty.
Let me not be forgotten, though the grave
  Has clasped its hideous arms around my brow.
Let me not be forgotten: though the wave of
  Time's dark current rolls above me now.
Yet not in tears remembered be my name;
  Weep over those ye loved; for me, for me,
Give me the wreath of glory, and let fame
  Over my tomb spread immortality.

Fanny Kemble achieved a measure of immortality in her autobiographical works and poetical-dramatic writings.

It takes the perception of a painter to see death and decay as 'beautiful and calming'. Gluck, one of this century's finest woman portrait and flower painters, wrote:

Reflections after a day painting . . .
I am living daily with death and decay,
and it is beautiful and calming. Something
Vital emanates – All is movement and
transubstantiation. Iridescent and nacreous
colours seem to float on my palette, and
then on to the canvas where they tremble
between opacity and translucence.

All order is lost; mechanics have gone
overboard – A phantasmagraphic irrelevance
links shapes and matter – A new world
evolves with increasing energy and freedom
soon to be invisibly reborn within our
airy envelope.

Death, immortality, rebirth, another life, give us much to ponder over in old age. To poet Christina Rossetti death was a blessed, peaceful sleep. She wrote this poem shortly before she died in 1894 when she was sixty-four years old.

Sleeping at last, the trouble and tumult over,
  Sleeping at last, the struggle and horror past,
Cold and white, out of sight of friends and of lover
  Sleeping at last.

No more a tired heart downcast or overcast,
  No more pangs that wring or shiftless fears that hover
Sleeping at last in a dreamless sleep locked fast.

Fast asleep. Singing birds in their leafy cover
  Cannot wake her, or shake her the gusty blast.
Under the purple thyme and the purple clover
  Sleeping at last.

Plate 14 'Seated Woman' by Grace Wheatley

Epilogue

The assembling of this collection of quotations from a wide range of distinguished British women over the centuries has given me immense pleasure and benefit. I hope that the anthology may give others the same pleasure and satisfaction it has given me, and may perhaps stimulate some to explore further the literary masterpieces of British women.

As a final tribute to them and to all women who have shaped and enriched our islands' history I would like to quote from a letter written by George Eliot to Emily Davies, the founder of Girton College, Cambridge, on 8 August 1868.

The spiritual wealth acquired for mankind by the difference of function founded on the other primary difference, and preparation that lies in woman's peculiar constitution [makes] for a precious moral influence. In the face of all wrongs, mistakes and failures, history had demonstrated that gain . . . We can no more afford to part with that exquisite type of gentleness, tenderness, possible maternity suffusing a woman's being with affectionateness which makes what we mean by the feminine character, than we can afford to part with human love . . . which is a growth and revelation beginning before all history.

Bibliography

Aldburghan, A., *Women in Print.* Writing Women and Womens' Magazines from the Restoration to the Accession of Victoria, Allen and Unwin 1972.

Asquith, M., *Countess of Oxford*, Off the Record, Frederick Muller 1943.

Astell, M., *A Serious Proposal to the Ladies for the Advancement of Their True and Greater Interest, in Two Parts by a Lover of Her Sex*, Printed for R. Wilkin at the King's Head in St Paul's Churchyard 1695.

Austen, J., *'Love and Friendship' and Other Early Works*, The Womens Press 1978.

Balcombe, J., and Phelps, R., *Selected writings of the Ingenious Mrs Aphra Behn*, Grove Press 1950.

Barrett, C., *Diaries and Letters of Madame D'Arblay Vols 1 & 2*, Swan & Soonerschein & Co 1893.

Behn, A., *The Dream*, The Penguin Book of Women Poets (eds) Carol Cosman, Joan Keefe, Kathleen Weaver, 1st in paperback 1979.

Behn, A., *The Fair Jilt, from Selected Writings of Mrs Aphra Behn*, edited by John Balcombe & Robert Phelps, Grove Press 1950.

Behn, A., *Preface to 'Lucky Chance'*, 1686.

Barrett Browning, E., *Aurora Leigh*, 1st published 1856.

Barrett Browning, E., *Glimpses into my own Life and Literary Character*, from Hitherto Unpublished Poems and Stories by E. Barrett Browning 1914.

Bigland, E., *The Indomitable Mrs Trollope*, 1953.

Blanch, L., *The Wilder Showes of Love*, Penguin Books 1959.

Bosanquet, G. (trans.), *Historia Nororum in Anglia*, Cresset Press 1964.

Bowen, S., *Drawn from Life, Reminiscences*, Collins 1941.

Braddon, M., *Lady Audley's Secret*, 1862.

Bradford, C. A., *Inscription*, from *Blanch Parry, Queen Elizabeth's Gentlewoman*, privately printed 1935.

Brendon, P., *Quotation from 'Eminent Edwardians'*, Penguin 1981.

Brittain, V., *Testament of Youth*, Victor Gollancz 1933.

Brittain, V., *Lady Into Woman: A History of Women from Victoria to Elizabeth*, Andrew Dakers 1953.

Bronte, C., *Jane Eyre*, 1st published 1847.

Bronte, C., *Shirley*, 1849.

Broughton, R., *Cometh Up as a Flower*, 1867.

Burgoyne, E., *Gertrude Bell 1889–1914 from her personal Papers*, Ernest Benn, London 1958.

Burney, F., *The Wanderer, or Female Difficulties*, 1814.

Burney, F., *Camilla*, 1st published 1796.

Burney, S., Introduction to *Diaries and Letters of Madame D'Arblay* Volume 1, *1778–84*, Swann and Sonnerschein & Co 1893.

Cameron, J., *Selected Writings*, Hogarth Press 1973.

Caufield, C., *The Emperor of the United States and other Magnificent British Eccentrics*, 1981.

Central Television., *Television Speech of Margaret Thatcher*, June 1986.

Chapman, R. W. (ed), *Jane Austen Selected Letters*, 1st published Oxford University Press 1955.

Chapman, R. W. (ed), *Jane Austen, Selected Letters*, Oxford University Press 1985.

Chicago, J., *The Dinner Party*, Anchor Books 1979.

Christie, A., *Unfinished Portrait*, Collins 1974.

Chudleigh, Lady, *To the Ladies*, Bernard Lintott 1701.

Cross, J. W., *George Eliot's Life as Related in her Letter and Journals*, William Blackwood & Sons 1885.

Crump, R. W., *A Birthday* by Christina Rossetti from *The Complete*

Poems of Christina Rossetti with Textual Notes, Louisiana State University Press 1979.

Drabble, M., *A Summer Bird Cage*, 1st published by Weidenfeld & Nicolson 1963.

Edgeworth, M., *Practical Education*, 1798.

Eliot, G., *Middlemarch*, 1st published 1872.

Elsted, E., *A Homily on the Birthday of St. Gregory*, 1709.

Fanshawe, H. C., *Memoirs of Lady Fanshawe*, John Lane 1907.

Ferrier, W., *The Life of Kathleen Ferrier*, Hamish Hamilton 1955.

Field, J., *A Life of Ones Own*, Chatto & Windus 1934.

Fiennes, C., *Through England on a Side-Saddle*, 1st published 1888.

Finch, A., Countess of Winchelsea, *Selected Poems* 1661–1720, Jon Cape 1928.

Finch, A., *Essay on Marriage*, Sidgwick & Jackson, London 1946.

Fonteyn, M., '*The Making of a Legend*', Collins 1973.

Forbes, B., *Ned's Girl, Dame Edith Evans*, Little, Brown & Co 1977.

Fry, E., *Observations on the Visiting Superintendence & Government of Female Prisoners*, 1827.

Fulford, R., *Your Dear Letter, Private Correspondence of Queen Victoria* to the Crown Princes of Prussia, 1865–1871, 1971.

Gaskell, Mrs., *Cranford*, 1st complete edition published 1853.

Gaskell, Mrs., *Wives and Daughters. An Everyday Story*, 1st published Cornhill 1866.

Gathorne-Hardy, R. (ed), *Ottoline at Garsington, Memoirs of Lady Ottoline Morrell*, 1st published Faber & Faber 1974.

Gluck, *Reflections after a day painting*, The Fine Arts Society 1980.

Haight, G. S., *Quotation from George Eliot a Biography*, Oxford University Press 1968.

Hall, R., *Marie Stopes, a Biography*, Virago 1978.

Halsbrond, R., *The Selected Letters of Lady Mary Montagu*, Oxford University Press 1956, Longman 1970.

Hays, M., *An Appeal to the Men of Great Britain on Behalf of the Women*, 1798.

Hepworth, Dame Barbara, *A Pictorial Autobiography*, Adams & Dart 1970.

Howard, C., *Mary Kingsley*, Hutchinson & Co 1937.

Ireland, Mrs Alexander, *Selections of the Letters of G. Ensor Jewsbury to Jane Welsh Carlyle*, Longmans 1892.

Kaum, J., *How Different from Us*, Bodley Head 1958.

Kegan Paul, C., *Mary Wollstonecraft's Letters to Imlay with prefatory memo*, Kegan Paul 1879.

Kemble, F., 'Let me not die,' The Collected Poems of F. Kemble, 1st published in Philadelphia 1844.

Kemble, F., *Records of Later Life Volume 1*, R Bentley & Son 1882.

Lawrence and E. M. Hanson, *The Four Brontes, the Lives & Works of Charlotte, Branwell, Emily and Ann Bronte*, Oxford University Press 1949.

Lehmann, R., *The Echoing Grove*, Collins 1953.

Lehmann, R., *The Swan in the Evening*, Collins 1967.

Lessing, D., *Children of Violence*, Penguin 1957, Panther Books 1967.

Lessing, D., *A Golden Notebook*, Penguin 1964.

Lessing, D., *Play with a Tiger*, Michael Joseph 1962 and Davis Poynter 1972.

Lessing, D., *Summer Before the Dark*, Jonathan Cape 1973.

Linder, L., *Journal of Beatrix Potter from 1881–1897*, Transcribed from her code writing, Frederick Warne & Co Ltd 1966.

Linton, E. L., *The Girl of the Period and other Social Essays*, R. Bentley & Son 1883.

Macaulay, R. (ed), *Letters to a Sister*, C. Babington-Smith, Collins 1964.

Macleod, S., *Letters from the Portuguese*, Secker & Warburg 1971.

Mansfield, K., *Her First Ball* from *Bliss and Other Stories*, Constable 1920, Penguin 1962.

Mansfield, K., '*The Flowering of the Self*,' The Journals of Katherine Mansfield, Constable 1954.

Mansfield, K., *Letters and Journals*, edited by C. K. Stead, Penguin 1977.

Martineau, H., *Autobiography Volume 1*, Smith & Elder Co 1877.

Martineau, H., *A Guide to the Lakes or Life in the Lake District*, 1950.

Mary Queen of Scots, *The Lives and Amours of Queens and Royal Mistresses*, 1726.

Meynell, A., *A Letter from a Girl to her Own Old Age*, from Poems of Alice Meynell, Oxford University Press 1940.

Middleton Murray, J., *Journal of Katherine Mansfield*, 1954.

Mitford, J., *Hons and Rebels*, Victor Gollancz 1960.

Mitford, M. R., *Our Village: Sketches of Rural Character & Scenery*, 1825.

Moers, E., *Contemporary Witness at Kit Cat Club London* in 17th Century, Quotation from *Liberary Women*, W. H. Allen & Co 1977.

Monk, W. H., *Hymns Ancient and Modern*, William Clowes & Sons 1845.

Morley, S., *Sybil Thorndike, A Life in the Theatre*, Weidenfeld & Nicolson 1977.

Murdoch, I., *The Sovereignty of Good*, The Leslie Stephen lecture, Cambridge University Press 1967.

Murray, M., *My First Hundred Years*, William Kimber 1963.

Newcastle, Margaret, Duchess of, *Poems, Opinions, Orations and Letters*, (ed), E. Jenkins 1872.

O'Brien, E., *A Pagan Place*, Faber 1973.

Paston, G., *Lady Mary Wortley Montagu and Her Times*, Methuen and Co 1984.

Peters, M., *Mrs Pat*, Bodley Head 1984.

Radcliffe, Mrs. A., *The Mysteries of Udolpho*, 1794.

Raine, K., *Amo Ergo Sum* from *The Year One*, Hamish Hamilton 1952.

Raverat, G., *Period Piece* A Cambridge Childhood, Faber & Faber 1952.

Reilly, C., *Scars Upon my Heart*, Women's poetry and verse of the First World War, Virago 1981.

Rhys, J., *Smile Please*, 1979.

Rosenberg, J., *Dorothy Richardson The Genius They Forgot*, Duckworth 1973.

Rossetti, G., *Monna Innominata* from Poems of Christina Rossetti, Macmillan, 1890.

Sackville West, V., *A Passenger to Teheran*, 1926.

Sanders, M. F., *The Life of Christina Rossetti*, Hutchinson

Sayers, D. L., *Unpopular Opinions*, Gollancz 1946.

Scott, S., *On Top of the World*, Hodder & Stoughton 1973.

Shelley, M., *Preface to Third Edition of Frankenstein*, 1st published 1818.

Showalter, E., *A Literature of Their Own*, Virago 1978.

Sidgwick, F., *The Complete Marjory Fleming, her Journals Letters & Verses* 1st pub. 1934.

Sitwell, E., *The British Eccentrics*, Faber & Faber 1933, Arrow Books 1960.

Sitwell, E., *Invocation from Green Song*, Macmillan & Co 1944.

Sitwell, E., *The Poet Laments the Coming of Old Age* taken from *Invocation from Green Song* (as above).

Smith, S., *Novel on Yellow Paper*, Jonathan Cape 1936.

Smyth, E., *Female Pipings in Eden*, Peter Davies 1933.

Spark, M., *Memento Mori*, Penguin Books 1961.

Stallworthy, J. (ed), *The Wife's Complaint*, Anon 10th Century verse from Anglo Saxon times, The Penguin Book of Love Poetry, 1985.

Stopes, M., *Married Love*, 1918.

Strickland, A., *Life of Queen Elizabeth I*, 1st published Dent & Sons 1906.

Terry, E., *Letter to George Bernard Shaw* from Ellen Terry & Bernard Shaw, a Correspondence, Constable & Co 1931, Reinhardt & Evans 1949.

Tynan, K., *Twenty-Five Years: Reminiscences*, Smith Elder & Co 1913.

Victorian Verse, (Anon).

Walters, C. (ed), *Revelations of Divine Love by Julian of Norwich*, Penguin Classics 1966.

Ward, Mrs H., *Robert Elsmere*, 1888.

Wickham, A., *The Fired Pot* and *Meditation at Kew* both taken from '*The Writings of Anna Wickham*, Virago Press 1984.

Wilkins, W. H., *The Romance of Isabel Lady Burton*, Hutchinson & Co 1897.

Wilson, P. W. C., *General Evangeline Booth of the Salvation Army*, Hodder & Stoughton 1948.

Wolley, H., *The Gentlewoman's Companion*, 1675

Wollstonecraft, M., *Mary and the Wrongs of Women*, 1798.

Wollstonecraft, M., *A Vindication for the Rights of Women*, 1792.

Wood, Mrs. H., *East Lynne* 1st published, Richard Bentley 1861.

Woolf, V., *Collected Essays*, Chatto & Windus 1966–69.

Woolf, V., *Old Mrs Grey*, Hogarth Press 1943.

Woolf, V., *Professions for Women* from Collected Essays, Hogarth Press 1931, Chatto & Windus 1966–69.

Woolf, V., *Three Guineas*, Hogarth Press 1938.

Woolf, V., *To The Lighthouse*, Penguin 1964.

Chronological table

1st Century		Queen Boudicea Boudicea led the final revolt against the Romans and was eventually defeated 60AD
5th to 11th Century		Anglo Saxon Era Hilda of Whitby presided over the Synod of Whitby assembled to decide the relative merits of Celtic and Roman Christianity 664AD
10th Century	Anon. Anglo Saxon Elegy Edith Matilda 1080–1118	The Norman Conquest 1066
14th Century	Lady Julian of Norwich 1342–14(20)	The Age of Chivalry characterised by the system of knighthood the worship of the Virgin Mary and reverence for women The Black Death 1348–9 Wycliffe's translation of the Bible 1382 William Caxton set up his printing press 1476
1500	Blanche Parry 1508–90	The Reformation 1547
	Queen Elizabeth 1 1533–1603	
	Mary Queen of Scots 1542–87	The reign of Queen Elizabeth I 1558–1603
1600	Margaret, Duchess of Newcastle 1617–73	

	Hannah Woolley 1623–77	
	Lady Ann Fanshawe 1625–80	
	Aphra Behn 1640–89	
	Lady Chudleigh 1656–1762	
	Ann Finch, Countess of Winchelsea 1661–1720	Nell Gwyn made her first appearance on the stage at Theatre Royal London. She exemplifies the recognition of women actresses 1665
	Celia Fiennes 1662–1741	
	Mary Astell 1668–1731	
	Elizabeth Elsted 1683–1765	
	Lady Mary Wortley Montagu 1689–1762	The reign of Queen Mary II and William of Orange 1689–94
	The Athenian Mercury Newspaper 1963	
1700	Lady Lawson 1700–1816	Queen Anne 1702–14
	Margaret Thompson 169– –1776	Parliament repealed the death penalty for 'witches' 1736
	Caroline Herschel 1750–1848	
	Susanna Burney b. 175–	
	Fanny Burney 1752–1840	
	Mary Wollstonecraft 1759–97	
	Mary Hays 1760–1843	
	Maria Cosway 1763–1823	
	Mrs. Ann Radcliffe 1764–1823	
	Maria Edgeworth 1767–1849	
	Cassandra Austen 1773–1845	
	Jane Austen 1775–1817	
	Elizabeth Fry 1780–1845	
	Frances Trollope 1780–1836	
	Mary Russell Mitford 1787–1855	
	Mary Shelley 1797–1851	The French Revolution 1791–1804

Chronological table

1800	Harriet Martineau 1802–76	
	Marjorie Fleming 1803–11	
	Sarah Adams 1805–48	
	Elizabeth Barrett Browning 1806–61	
	Jane Digby 1807–81	
	Fanny Kemble 1809–93	
	Mrs. Elizabeth Gaskell 1810–65	
	Geraldine Jewsbury 1812–80	
	Julia Cameron 1815–79	
	Charlotte Bronte 1816–55	
	Emily Bronte 1818–48	
	George Eliot (Mary Anne Evans) 1819–80	
	Queen Victoria 1819–1901	
	Anne Bronte 1820–49	
	Florence Nightingale 1820–1910	
	Eliza Lynn Linton 1822–98	
	Francis Mary Buss 1827–94	
	Christina Rossetti 1830–94	
	Isabel Burton 1831–96	
	Dorothea Beale 1831–1906	The reign of Queen Victoria 1837–1901
		Infant Custody Bill passed, campaigned by Caroline Norton 1839
	Rhoda Broughton 1840–1920	Elizabeth Fry founded a Home for training nurses 1840
	Alice Meynell 1847–1922	
1850	Mrs. Humphrey Ward 1851–1920	The Crimean War 1854
		Divorce Bill and First Married Womens Property Bill campaigned by Caroline Norton 1857
	Emmeline Pankhurst 1858–1928	

Mrs. Beatrice Webb 1858–1943	
Ethel Smyth 1858–1944	Publication of Florence Nightingale's 'Notes on Nursing' raising the standards and status of the nursing profession 1859
Katherine Tynan 1861–1931	
Beatrix Potter 1861–1943	Publication of Mrs. Beeton's 'Household Management' 1861 the first book on cookery and domestic science 1861
Mary Kingsley 1862–1900	
Margaret Murray 1863–1963	
Margot Asquith 1864–1945	
Mrs. Patrick Campbell 1865–1940	
Evangeline Booth 1865–1950	
Maude Gonne 1866–1953	
Gertrude Bell 1868–1926	Publication of John Stuart Mill's 'The subjection of Women' advocating women's rights 1869 Elizabeth Garret registered as the first British woman doctor 1869 The Elementary Education Act 1870
Eleanor Rathbone 1872–1946	
Lady Ottoline Morell 1873–1938	
Dorothy Richardson 1873–1957	
Gwen John 1876–1939	
Edith Sitwell 1877–1964	
Lady Edna Clarke-Hall 1879–1979	
Marie Stopes 1880–1958	
Rose Macaulay 1881–1958	

	Jessie Pope 18– –1941	
	Virginia Woolf 1882–1941	
	Sylvia Pankhurst 1882–1960	
	Sybil Thorndike 1882–1976	
	Gwendolen Raverat 1885–1957	Repeal of The Contagious Diseases Act of 1866–9 campaigned against by Josephine Butler
	Katherine Mansfield 1888–1923	
	Grace Whealtley 1888–1970	
	Dame Edith Evans 1888–1976	
	Enid Bangnold 1889–1981	
	Agatha Christie 1890–1976	
	Vita Sackville West 1892–1962	
	Stella Bowen 1893–1947	
	Vera Brittain 1893–1970	
	Dorothy L. Sayers 1893–1957	
	Jean Rhys 1894–1979	
	Gluck 1895–	
1900	Joanna Field 1900–	The death of Queen Victoria 1901
	Stevie Smith 1902–71	
	Barbara Hepworth 1903–75	
	Rosamund Lehmann 1903–	The Suffragette Movement 1906–14
	Margaret Barker 1907–	
	Anne Finch 1908–	
	Kathleen Raine 1908–	
	Kathleen Ferrier 1912–53	The first World War 1914–18
	Jessica Mitford 1917–	
	Muriel Spark 1918–	Representation of Peoples Act passed granting enfranchisement for women householders over 30 years of age 1918
	Dame Iris Murdoch 1919–	
	Doris Lessing 1919–	

Margot Fonteyn 1919–	Lady Nancy Astor elected the first woman member of Parliament 1919
	Britain's first Birth Control Ciinic opened 1921
Margaret Thatcher 1925–	
Sheila Scott 1927–	Voting for parliament granted to all British Citizens over 21 years 1928
	The founding of the Family Planning Association 1930
Edna O'Brien 1932–	
Margaret Drabble 1939–	
Sheila Macleod 1939–	The Accession to the throne of Queen Elizabeth II 1952
	Rose Heilbron took silk and became the first woman recorder in the UK and Queen's Counsellor 1956
	Elizabeth Lanc became the first woman Judge in England 1965
	Margaret Thatcher MP became first woman Prime Minister of Britain 1979
	Act passed to enable women to be ordinated Deacons of the Church of England 1986

Index